The Vocabulary Diet

Book Two

The Vocabulary Diet

Book Two

Dave DeRocco

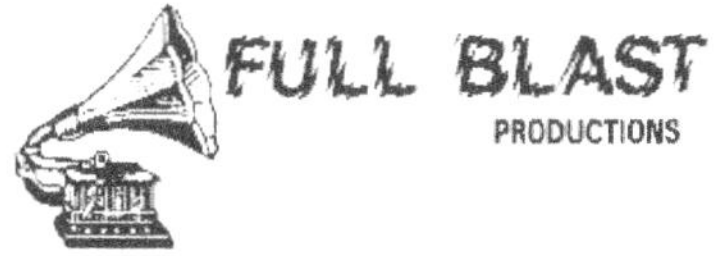

IN CANADA   IN THE UNITED STATES

FB Productions   FB Productions
Box 408   Box 1297
Virgil, Ontario   Lewiston, New York 14092-8297
L0S 1T0

Phone: 905-468-7558
Fax: 905-468-5706
E-mail: fbp@vaxxine.com
Website: www.fullblastproductions.com

National Library of Canada Cataloguing in Publication Data

DeRocco, David, 1961-
    The vocabulary diet

ISBN 1-895451-42-6 (bk. 1) - ISBN 1-895451-43-4 (bk. 2) -
ISBN 1-895451-44-2 (bk.3)

1. English Language -- Textbooks for second language learners.
2. Vocabulary. I. Title.

PE1449.D47 2001   428.2' 4   C2001-903113-0

Printed in Canada.

ISBN 1-895451-43-4

INTRODUCTION

The Vocabulary Diet is a three book series of reproducible lessons designed to increase an intermediate/advanced level ESL student's vocabulary. Each book contains thirty units, with five words featured in each unit. Every unit is two pages long, and a **complete answer key** has been included for each lesson. **The Vocabulary Diet** is effective not only because it allows students to be presented with the new vocabulary items in a variety of exercises and in many contexts but it also works because the opportunity for repeated exposure is built in and because students are required to consider and manipulate the new words in several different ways.

Words chosen for inclusion and the units in **The Vocabulary Diet** are not graded. The words are not grouped because of any similarity of meaning. The words included were chosen at random based on the author's belief that being able to use them will enhance a learner's ability to speak effectively.

When using **The Vocabulary Diet** it is recommended that every student has access to a dictionary and a thesaurus. Teachers should determine, taking their students' language level into consideration, whether new vocabulary words should be looked up in the dictionary before proceeding to the actual lessons in the book.

Every unit in **The Vocabulary Diet** begins with **three sample sentences for each word** being studied. The students are then given five possible meanings for each word and by working with context clues the students must determine the word that is the most suitable definition.

Next the students are given a **fill-in-the-blanks exercise**. Five sentences are given with the student's responsibitlity being to place the correct vocabulary word in the correct sentence.

Following this is a **synonym matching exercise**. The five vocabulary words are given along with a list of five other words. The vocabulary word must be matched with its closest synonym.

There is a **sentence building exercise**. Single words or groups of words, including the vocabulary words, are given and the students must arrange the scrambled words to form proper sentences.

Finally, there is a **word elimination exercise**. Students are given five potential synonyms for the vocabulary words being studied. Only three of the words are true synonyms. The students must identify which two words are not synonyms.

Repetition is the key to successful vocabulary learning. **The Vocabulary Diet** provides that repetition. A good teacher will not cease reinforcing new vocabulary with what is presented on these pages. Get your students to use their new words by **creating their own sentences**. Get your students to pretend they are reporters and to go out and survey English speakers to see if the native speakers can come up with definitions or synonyms for the vocabulary words. **The Vocabulary Diet** aims to make learning an enjoyable and fruitful experience for your students.

THE VOCABULARY DIET: UNIT 1

1) *aid* (noun)

Examples:
a)   The students applied for financial aid to help pay for their college tuition.
b)   The United Nations agreed to supply humanitarian aid to the refugees.
c)   Aid from neighboring countries arrived in Italy after the earthquake.

Circle the correct meaning:

a) bandage   b) food   c) help   d) troops   e) admirers

2) *sour* (adjective)

Examples:
a)   They could tell by the sour look on the waiter's face he was not going to be friendly.
b)   Nancy had a sour attitude towards any vegetable that was not cooked before being served.
c)   Alan had a sour opinion about the proposal to put a highway through his neighborhood.

Circle the correct meaning:

a) disagreeable   b) surprised   c) supportive   d) helpful   e) warm

3) *suspicious* (adjective)

Examples:
a)   Neighbors reported suspicious behavior at Mr. Blake's house the night he disappeared.
b)   Rodney had suspicious feelings that his new employee was stealing money from the cash register.
c)   "Don't get any suspicious ideas about my work," warned Dr. Frankenstein.

Circle the correct meaning:

a) additional   b) intense   c) confident   d) distrustful   e) pleasant

4) *isolation* (noun)

Examples:
a)   Samples of the anthrax virus were placed in isolation in a guarded laboratory for further testing.
b)   The prisoner was ordered to endure four weeks of isolation as punishment for bad behavior.
c)   Hakim knew the isolation of being the only boy in classroom full of girls.

Circle the correct meaning:

a) companionship   b) togetherness   c) belonging   d) display   e) separation

5) *tousled* (adjective)

Examples:
a)   Phillip was disgusted by the tousled condition of his apartment after his birthday party.
b)   Marjory always had tousled hair when she first climbed out of bed in the morning.
c)   Police were searching for a homeless man in tousled clothes.

Circle the correct meaning:

a) proper   b) messy   c) impeccable   d) coordinated   e) stylish

FILL IN THE BLANKS:

Below are five sentences. Each contains a blank. Fill in the blank by using the appropriate word from this unit. Each word is used only once.

1) Sailors often experience a feeling of _________________ after spending months at sea.
2) Julia was growing _________________ of her new boyfriend.
3) The electrician discovered a ball of _________________ wiring hooked up to the fuse box.
4) The recital was ruined by the _________________ notes coming from the out of tune piano.
5) The social worker offered Diane financial _________________ to help feed her three children.

SYNONYM MATCHING:

On the left are words from this unit. Draw a line to the word on the right with the closest meaning.

1) aid   a) unpleasant
2) sour   b) seclusion
3) suspicious   c) disheveled
4) isolation   d) questionable
5) tousled   e) assistance

SENTENCE BUILDING:

Assemble the scrambled clues below to form proper sentences.

1) all citizens to/of the victims/The President asked/come to the aid
2) suspicious looking people/to the principal/The teacher asked/report any/students to
3) Kenny asked/tousled suit jacket/his mom/to iron his/to the party/wear it/so he could
4) space travel/Astronauts had to/to prepare for/in isolation/spend months
5) the unexpected attacks/Negotiations turned/sour after/on the United States

WORD ELIMINATION:

Words from this unit are on the left. Five possible synonyms for each word are given below. Only three of the words are true synonyms. Circle the two words that do not belong.

1) aid	a) criticism	b) expenses	c) support	d) relief	e) funding
2) sour	a) offensive	b) sweet	c) unlikable	d) lovable	e) nasty
3) suspicious	a) trustful	b) skeptical	c) disbelieving	d) doubtful	e) honest
4) isolation	a) separation	b) remoteness	c) group	d) shared	e) segregation
5) tousled	a) tangled	b) neat	c) tidy	d) ruffled	e) windswept

---

ANSWER KEY:

CIRCLE THE CORRECT MEANING: 1) c 2) a 3) d 4) e 5) b
FILL IN THE BLANKS: 1) isolation 2) suspicious 3) tousled 4) sour 5) aid
SYNONYM MATCHING: 1) e 2) a 3) d 4) b 5) c
SENTENCE BUILDING:
1) The President asked all citizens to come to the aid of the victims.
2) The teacher asked students to report any suspicious looking people to the principal.
3) Kenny asked his mom to iron his tousled suit jacket so he could wear it to the party.
4) Astronauts had to spend months in isolation to prepare for space travel.
5) Negotiations turned sour after the unexpected attacks on the United States.
WORD ELIMINATION:
1) a,b 2) b,d 3) a,e 4) c,d 5) b,c

1) *cheap* (adjective)

Examples:
a)   Damien quit his job because his boss was too cheap to give him a raise in pay.
b)   Jack walked five miles to work every day because he was too cheap to pay for a bus ride.
c)   Amber was cheap with her money and she never spent a dime on her friends.

Circle the correct meaning:

a) generous   b) giving   c) proud   d) miserly   e) wealthy

2) *vague* (adjective)

Examples:
a)   Gary got lost after following the vague directions he was given to the cottage.
b)   The witness was vague about exact dates and times relating to the crime.
c)   The vague instructions provided in the box made it difficult to assemble the bookshelf.

Circle the correct meaning:

a) accurate   b) detailed   c) descriptive   d) extensive   e) unclear

3) *unorthodox* (adjective)

Examples:
a)   Dr. Wilson's methods were highly unorthodox but they proved to be very effective.
b)   Bradley's teaching style was considered too unorthodox for children in the first grade.
c)   Putting a hamburger into a toaster is certainly an unorthodox way to cook it.

Circle the correct meaning:

a) unusual   b) inventive   c) brilliant   d) impressive   e) interesting

4) *journey* (noun)

Examples:
a)   Christopher Columbus made the long journey to America in 1492.
b)   Mountain climbers must pack proper supplies to make a successful journey up Mount Everest.
c)   Karen was looking forward to her journey across the Atlantic Ocean to visit cousins in England.

Circle the correct meaning:

a) reservation   b) trip   c) comment   d) view   e) observation

5) *catch* (noun)

Examples:
a)   The only catch to Paul's plan to sail around the world was the fact he did not own a boat!
b)   Hitting an iceberg was a catch the captain of the Titanic did not expect.
c)   When Marlee saw the sign advertising free furniture she knew there had to be a catch.

Circle the correct meaning:

a) haul   b) contain   c) hitch   d) solution   e) explanation

FILL IN THE BLANKS:

Below are five sentences. Each contains a blank. Fill in the blank by using the appropriate word from this unit. Each word is used only once.

1) The professor asked Gail to clarify her answer because he felt it was too ___________________.
2) Cindy believed her ___________________ style of dress was a good way to get noticed.
3) The trip to Banff included a long ___________________ through the ice fields.
4) Larry worried that an unexpected ___________________ might delay the sale of his house.
5) Kendra's grandfather was too ___________________ to buy himself the glasses he needed.

SYNONYM MATCHING:

On the left are words from this unit. Draw a line to the word on the right with the closest meaning.

1) cheap	a) alternative
2) vague	b) expedition
3) unorthodox	c) stumbling block
4) journey	d) penny-pinching
5) catch	e) imprecise

SENTENCE BUILDING:

Assemble the scrambled clues below to form proper sentences.

1) was considered cheap/worth less than/Giving a/one hundred dollars/wedding gift
2) tired of hearing/vague opinions/about politics/the professor's/The students grew
3) journey to Mars/make the long/Scientists believe/humans will eventually
4) There was always/that Freddie made/any plan/a catch to/for his friends
5) to wrestle/Encouraging a man/is an unorthodox/way to/test his courage/an alligator

WORD ELIMINATION:

Words from this unit are on the left. Five possible synonyms for each word are given below. Only three of the words are true synonyms. Circle the two words that do not belong.

1) cheap	a) tightfisted	b) grudging	c) wealthy	d) glowing	e) stingy
2) vague	a) ambiguous	b) pointed	c) indefinite	d) direct	e) confusing
3) unorthodox	a) plain	b) expected	c) strange	d) odd	e) irregular
4) journey	a) voyage	b) excursion	c) individual	d) tour	e) appointment
5) catch	a) clue	b) drawback	c) snag	d) answer	e) obstacle

ANSWER KEY:

CIRCLE THE CORRECT MEANING: 1) d 2) e 3) a 4) b 5) c
FILL IN THE BLANKS: 1) vague 2) unorthodox 3) journey 4) catch 5) cheap
SYNONYM MATCHING: 1) d 2) e 3) a 4) b 5) c
SENTENCE BUILDING:
1) Giving a wedding gift worth less than one hundred dollars was considered cheap.
2) The students grew tired of hearing the professor's vague opinions about politics.
3) Scientists believe humans will eventually make the long journey to Mars.
4) There was always a catch to any plan that Freddie made for his friends.
5) Encouraging a man to wrestle an alligator is an unorthodox way to test his courage.
WORD ELIMINATION:
1) c,d 2) b,d 3) a,b 4) c,e 5) a,d

1) *class* (noun)

Examples:
a)   Fans of the British royal family loved Princess Diana for the class she displayed in public.
b)   Even though she was poor Margaret had a sense of class all her own.
c)   Friends admired Cynthia for the class she displayed in difficult situations.

Circle the correct meaning:

a) refinement   b) anger   c) laughter   d) wealth   e) crudeness

2) *barricade* (noun)

Examples:
a)   Police set up a barricade to stop the angry mob from entering the building.
b)   A barricade was built around the castle to keep the peasants away from the King.
c)   The zoo installed a solid steel barricade to keep the rhinoceros away from the elephants.

Circle the correct meaning:

a) passage   b) hallway   c) opening   d) fence   e) doorway

3) *peculiar* (adjective)

Examples:
a)   Ian looked rather peculiar in his bright yellow pants and purple shirt.
b)   Martha was considered a peculiar woman because she never came outside during the day.
c)   Craig had a peculiar habit of clicking his teeth when he took a drink.

Circle the correct meaning:

a) decent   b) friendly   c) common   d) remarkable   e) odd

4) *tiny* (adjective)

Examples:
a)   The truck seemed rather tiny compared to the giant airplane.
b)   A tiny mouse had chewed through the wires running into the cottage.
c)   Customers were disappointed by the tiny portions of food served at the restaurant.

Circle the correct meaning:

a) gigantic   b) small   c) colossal   d) lengthy   e) different

5) *trash* (noun)

Examples:
a)   Volunteer crews were asked to clean up trash left in the streets after the parade.
b)   Strong winds were blowing trash all over the neighborhood.
c)   The kids were searching through the trash looking for bottles they could recycle.

Circle the correct meaning:

a) treasure   b) supplies   c) garbage   d) paper   e) boxes

THE VOCABULARY DIET: UNIT 3

FILL IN THE BLANKS:

Below are five sentences. Each contains a blank. Fill in the blank by using the appropriate word from this unit. Each word is used only once.

1) Visitors to the campground were surprised to find a ___________________ blocking their entry.
2) Raccoons tipped over the garbage can looking for food scraps in the ___________________.
3) The princess slipped her foot into the ___________________ glass slipper.
4) Dylan showed a lot of ___________________ when he offered his seat to the elderly woman.
5) There was a ___________________ odor coming from behind the house.

SYNONYM MATCHING:

On the left are words from this unit. Draw a line to the word on the right with the closest meaning.

1) class		a) blockade
2) barricade		b) minute
3) peculiar		c) debris
4) tiny		d) elegance
5) trash		e) irregular

SENTENCE BUILDING:

Assemble the scrambled clues below to form proper sentences.

1) she was rich/class her/friends thought/with such/Amber always dressed
2) used to/enemy barricade/destroy the/Explosives were
3) when it/was played/sounded peculiar/The guitar was/and it/not properly tuned
4) tiny bubbles/The ginger ale/was full of/in the glass
5) It was Dani's/every morning/the trash out/job to take/before school

WORD ELIMINATION:

Words from this unit are on the left. Five possible synonyms for each word are given below. Only three of the words are true synonyms. Circle the two words that do not belong.

1) class	a) aroma	b) conflict	c) style	d) dignity	e) flair
2) barricade	a) fortification	b) wall	c) line	d) doorway	e) barrier
3) peculiar	a) fancy	b) strange	c) weird	d) unusual	e) ordinary
4) tiny	a) large	b) little	c) sizeable	d) petite	e) teeny
5) trash	a) waste	b) heirloom	c) rubbish	d) jewel	e) litter

ANSWER KEY:

CIRCLE THE CORRECT MEANING: 1) a 2) d 3) e 4) b 5) c
FILL IN THE BLANKS: 1) barricade 2) trash 3) tiny 4) class 5) peculiar
SYNONYM MATCHING: 1) d 2) a 3) e 4) b 5) c
SENTENCE BUILDING:
1) Amber always dressed with such class her friends thought she was rich.
2) Explosives were used to destroy the enemy barricade.
3) The guitar was not properly tuned and it sounded peculiar when it was played.
4) The ginger ale in the glass was full of tiny bubbles.
5) It was Dani's job to take the trash out every morning before school.
WORD ELIMINATION:
1) a,b 2) c,d 3) a,e 4) a,c 5) b,d

1) *combination* (noun)

Examples:
a)   The right combination of pitching and hitting helped the Diamondbacks beat the Yankees.
b)   Luke lost all of his savings through a combination of bad luck and poor investment.
c)   Steak and lobster is a popular dinner combination of meat and seafood.

Circle the correct meaning:

a) separation   b) division   c) blend   d) menu   e) talent

2) *just* (adjective)

Examples:
a)   Mrs. Wilson felt it was a just decision to make Dennis pay for the window he broke.
b)   Many people believe life in prison is a just punishment for a person convicted of murder.
c)   Drake was a just lawyer who worked hard for people wrongly accused of a crime.

Circle the correct meaning:

a) awkward   b) fair   c) confusing   d) legal   e) immoral

3) *reckless* (adjective)

Examples:
a)   It is considered very reckless behavior to play on railway tracks.
b)   Police determined that reckless driving was the cause of the accident.
c)   Mrs. Chong told her son he was being reckless by riding double on a bicycle.

Circle the correct meaning:

a) exciting   b) brave   c) daring   d) irresponsible   e) courageous

4) *value* (noun)

Examples:
a)   A knowledge of computers is of great value in this job.
b)   After taking the car for a test drive Marilyn decided its value was overstated by the salesperson.
c)   The art expert set the value of the Picasso painting at twenty million dollars.

Circle the correct meaning:

a) history   b) weight   c) size   d) width   e) worth

5) *hope* (noun)

Examples:
a)   Seeing her niece get married was always Aunt Fran's greatest hope.
b)   It is the hope of people around the world that a peaceful solution can be reached in the Middle East.
c)   Families of the sailors lost at sea maintained hope that the missing ship would be found.

Circle the correct meaning:

a) desire   b) fear   c) loathing   d) result   e) togetherness

THE VOCABULARY DIET: UNIT 4

FILL IN THE BLANKS:

Below are five sentences. Each contains a blank. Fill in the blank by using the appropriate word from this unit. Each word is used only once.

1) The teacher expressed ___________________ that all her students would pass the exam.
2) Jumping over a row of buses on a motorcycle is still considered a ___________________ stunt.
3) It was hard to determine the ___________________ of the products on sale in the store.
4) The boxer threw a steady ___________________ of punches with his left and right hands.
5) President Bush was being ___________________ when he offered aid to the Afghan people.

SYNONYM MATCHING:

On the left are words from this unit. Draw a line to the word on the right with the closest meaning.

1) combination   a) wish
2) just   b) cost
3) reckless   c) honorable
4) value   d) mixture
5) hope   e) careless

SENTENCE BUILDING:

Assemble the scrambled clues below to form proper sentences.

1) style and grace/Princess Diana/combination of/had a unique
2) a just war/there is no/Anti-war/demonstrators believe/such thing as
3) Stacey felt/reckless hobby/that going/an extremely/skydiving was
4) for the racehorse/a suitable value/not agree upon/The jockeys could
5) a handsome prince/Her only hope/she would meet/was that

WORD ELIMINATION:

Words from this unit are on the left. Five possible synonyms for each word are given below. Only three of the words are true synonyms. Circle the two words that do not belong.

1) combination   a) individual   b) fusion   c) singular   d) assortment   e) grouping
2) just   a) impartial   b) righteous   c) crooked   d) reasonable   e) biased
3) reckless   a) cautious   b) negligent   c) foolish   d) crazy   e) careful
4) value   a) worth   b) charge   c) amount   d) change   e) insignificant
5) hope   a) aspiration   b) disbelief   c) dream   d) nonsense   e) plan

ANSWER KEY:

CIRCLE THE CORRECT MEANING: 1) c 2) b 3) d 4) e 5) a
FILL IN THE BLANKS: 1) hope 2) reckless 3) value 4) combination 5) just
SYNONYM MATCHING: 1) d 2) c 3) e 4) b 5) a
SENTENCE BUILDING:
1) Princess Diana had a unique combination of style and grace.
2) Anti-war demonstrators believe there is no such thing as a just war.
3) Stacey felt that going skydiving was an extremely reckless hobby.
4) They jockeys could not agree upon a suitable value for the racehorse.
5) Her only hope was that she would meet a handsome prince.
WORD ELIMINATION:
1) a,c 2) c,e 3) a,e 4) d,e 5) b,d

1) *report* (noun)

Examples:
a)   The television crew filed a report direct from the scene of the car accident.
b)   "I want your report on my desk by tomorrow morning," demanded Laura's boss.
c)   The report from the city recommended a new stoplight be installed at the corner of Arthur Street.

Circle the correct meaning:

a) account   b) picture   c) department   d) instruction   e) speech

2) *scarce* (adjective)

Examples:
a)   People were getting sick because medicine was in scarce supply.
b)   Fans were scarce at the ballpark because of the threat of rain.
c)   Jobs were scarce during the Great Depression due to the poor economy.

Circle the correct meaning:

a) abundant   b) limited   c) plentiful   d) generous   e) large

3) *affection* (noun)

Examples:
a)   The children showed their affection by hugging the happy puppy.
b)   Bianca was a charming woman with a genuine affection for life.
c)   The President kissed his wife in a tender moment of affection.

Circle the correct meaning:

a) disdain   b) hatred   c) love   d) cruelty   e) curious

4) *boring* (adjective)

Examples:
a)   Film critics wrote that the movie was long and boring.
b)   Dick was not impressed with the boring speech given at the meeting.
c)   The party was very boring because the kids were not allowed to play music.

Circle the correct meaning:

a) exciting   b) thrilling   c) enjoyable   d) dull   e) fun

5) *pillar* (noun)

Examples:
a)   The carpenter was called to replace the rotted wooden pillar holding up the roof.
b)   A crumbling pillar was all that remained of the ancient castle.
c)   The bride was photographed standing next to a pillar in the church.

Circle the correct meaning:

a) floor   b) brick   c) pillow   d) door   e) pole

THE VOCABULARY DIET: UNIT 5

FILL IN THE BLANKS:

Below are five sentences. Each contains a blank. Fill in the blank by using the appropriate word from this unit. Each word is used only once.

1) The students were forced to sit through another _________________ lecture by the professor.
2) David began to show Marlee a lot of _________________ during her pregnancy.
3) Bill wanted to make sure the _________________ had been installed properly.
4) According to the police _________________ the suspect had blonde hair and blue eyes.
5) Tickets to the U2 concert at the coliseum were _________________ .

SYNONYM MATCHING:

On the left are words from this unit. Draw a line to the word on the right with the closest meaning.

1) report	a) in short supply
2) scarce	b) uninteresting
3) affection	c) post
4) boring	d) friendliness
5) pillar	e) story

SENTENCE BUILDING:

Assemble the scrambled clues below to form proper sentences.

1) the other documents/Michael completed/filed it with/his report and
2) desert climates/usually very/Water is/scarce in
3) The counselor/to his children/told him/more affection/to display
4) boring lives/often lead/try new things/afraid to/People who are
5) ballroom floor/A stunning/above the/copper pillar/rose high

WORD ELIMINATION:

Words from this unit are on the left. Five possible synonyms for each word are given below. Only three of the words are true synonyms. Circle the two words that do not belong.

1) report	a) statement	b) commentary	c) gift	d) description	e) union
2) scarce	a) ample	b) lavish	c) insufficient	d) meager	e) sparse
3) affection	a) fondness	b) disbelief	c) spite	d) warmth	e) devotion
4) boring	a) tedious	b) dreary	c) anxious	d) awesome	e) tiresome
5) pillar	a) space	b) support	c) column	d) solid	e) upright

ANSWER KEY:

CIRCLE THE CORRECT MEANING: 1) a 2) b 3) c 4) d 5) e
FILL IN THE BLANKS: 1) boring 2) affection 3) pillar 4) report 5) scarce
SYNONYM MATCHING: 1) e 2) a 3) d 4) b 5) c
SENTENCE BUILDING:

1) Michael completed his report and filed it with the other documents.
2) Water is usually very scarce in desert climates.
3) The counselor told him to display more affection to his children.
4) People who are afraid to try new things often lead boring lives.
5) A stunning copper pillar rose high above the ballroom floor.

WORD ELIMINATION:

1) c,e 2) a,b 3) b,c 4) c,d 5) a,d

1) *technique* (noun)

Examples:
a)   Elvis Stojko received top marks for his skating technique in the competition.
b)   The doctors at Sick Kids Hospital were attempting a new technique for treating cancer.
c)   The baseball coach was impressed by the new pitching technique Roger was using.

Circle the correct meaning:

a) fashion   b) agreement   c) practice   d) blunder   e) method

2) *rip* (noun)

Examples:
a)   A huge rip in the parachute caused the accident that injured the stunt man.
b)   Billy asked his mother to sew the rip in his pants.
c)   No one would buy the painting because of the rip in the canvas.

Circle the correct meaning:

a) mend   b) seam   c) tear   d) cuff   e) pocket

3) *dwelling* (noun)

Examples:
a)   The family was in need of a new dwelling after fire destroyed their home.
b)   The college students were hoping to share a small dwelling during the school months.
c)   The cottage was only used as a family dwelling during the summer months.

Circle the correct meaning:

a) residence   b) hovel   c) kitchen   d) meal   e) gathering

4) *drop* (noun)

Examples:
a)   The Chicago Bulls suffered a drop in attendance after Michael Jordan retired.
b)   A sudden drop in interest rates made it more affordable to buy a house.
c)   The company reported a drop in revenue after the attacks on New York City.

Circle the correct meaning:

a) increase b) rise c) elevation d) decrease e) addition

5) *kind* (noun)

Examples:
a)   Pepsi was the only kind of soft drink Marlee would drink.
b)   The store did not stock that particular kind of footwear.
c)   The recipe required a special kind of flour in order to make the cookies.

Circle the correct meaning:

a) compliment   b) type   c) duplicate   d) clone   e) size

FILL IN THE BLANKS:

Below are five sentences. Each contains a blank. Fill in the blank by using the appropriate word from this unit. Each word is used only once.

1) There was a sudden _________________ in the value of the real estate market.
2) They used the cave as a temporary _________________ during the rain storm.
3) The latex paint was not the _________________ of paint Ginger had ordered from the store.
4) The sharp metal edge had caused a _________________ in the skin on Steve's hand.
5) The hardware store was teaching customers a new _________________ to install carpet.

SYNONYM MATCHING:

On the left are words from this unit. Draw a line to the word on the right with the closest meaning.

1) technique   a) reduction
2) rip   b) lodging
3) dwelling   c) procedure
4) drop   d) brand
5) kind   e) slit

SENTENCE BUILDING:

Assemble the scrambled clues below to form proper sentences.

1) insisted his/their technique/students improve/The karate instructor
2) in the sail/They could not/of a rip/sailboat because/use the
3) The box was/keep ten puppies/not a suitable/in which to/dwelling
4) price of gas/No one would/the rapid drop/in the/have predicted
5) which kind of/him to buy/ice cream his/wife had asked/Kevin forgot

WORD ELIMINATION:

Words from this unit are on the left. Five possible synonyms for each word are given below. Only three of the words are true synonyms. Circle the two words that do not belong.

1) technique   a) unskilled   b) unable   c) style   d) system   e) way
2) rip   a) slash   b) gash   c) stitch   d) split   e) repair
3) dwelling   a) house   b) transient   c) home   d) mobile   e) abode
4) drop   a) rise   b) decline   c) fall   d) slump   e) climb
5) kind   a) sort   b) class   c) false   d) imposter   e) variety

---

ANSWER KEY:

CIRCLE THE CORRECT MEANING: 1) e 2) c 3) a 4) d 5) b
FILL IN THE BLANKS: 1) drop 2) dwelling 3) kind 4) rip 5) technique
SYNONYM MATCHING: 1) c 2) e 3) b 4) a 5) d
SENTENCE BUILDING:
1) The karate instructor insisted his students improve their technique.
2) They could not use the sailboat because of a rip in the sail.
3) The box was not a suitable dwelling in which to keep ten puppies.
4) No one would have predicted the rapid drop in the price of gas.
5) Kevin forgot which kind of ice cream his wife had asked him to buy.
WORD ELIMINATION:
1) a,b 2) c,e 3) b,d 4) a,e 5) c,d

1) *staff* (noun)

Examples:
a)   The radio station fired fifteen of its staff in an attempt to cut costs and reduce expenses.
b)   The furniture store was well known for having the most helpful staff in the city.
c)   The students were hired on as temporary staff for the summer.

Circle the correct meaning:

a) rigid   b) workers   c) foundation   d) customers   e) clients

2) *sociable* (adjective)

Examples:
a)   The employment agency was looking for sociable people to work in customer service.
b)   Christine's classmates voted her "the most sociable girl in school".
c)   Mike had the flu and did not feel very sociable when he got to work.

Circle the correct meaning:

a) angry   b) miserable   c) friendly   d) distant   e) quiet

3) *goal* (noun)

Examples:
a)   Winning the championship was the number one goal of the professional football team.
b)   Stephen's goal was to climb Mount Everest before his 40th birthday.
c)   Finding a peaceful solution to the crisis was the main goal of the coalition.

Circle the correct meaning:

a) purpose   b) score   c) obstruction   d) cause   e) effect

4) *ground* (noun)

Examples:
a)   The ground was covered with fallen tree branches after the rainstorm.
b)   The farmer buried the dead fox deep in the ground so no other animals would dig it up.
c)   The plane hit the ground and exploded on impact.

Circle the correct meaning:

a) air   b) carpet   c) liquid   d) earth   e) structure

5) *hurdle* (noun)

Examples:
a)   Getting past the customs agents was the last hurdle faced by the smugglers.
b)   Having asthma should not be a hurdle for young athletes training for a career in sports.
c)   Getting a permit to build is often a hurdle for construction companies.

Circle the correct meaning:

a) companion   b) disease   c) pillar   d) checkpoint   e) obstacle

THE VOCABULARY DIET: UNIT 7

FILL IN THE BLANKS:
Below are five sentences. Each contains a blank. Fill in the blank by using the appropriate word from this unit. Each word is used only once.

1) Kelly tried to be _________________ with Vince even though she didn't like him.
2) The car accident was an unexpected _________________ to the traveler's plans.
3) Marsha was impressed with the service provided by the hotel _________________.
4) The marketing department set a sales _________________ of 10 million units.
5) The _________________ was frozen, making it impossible to dig holes for the fence.

SYNONYM MATCHING:
On the left are words from this unit. Draw a line to the word on the right with the closest meaning.

1) staff	a) ambition
2) sociable	b) land
3) goal	c) welcoming
4) ground	d) workforce
5) hurdle	e) snag

SENTENCE BUILDING:
Assemble the scrambled clues below to form proper sentences.

1) job well done/The company president/bonus for a/his staff a/gave every one of
2) The dance was/a sociable event/designed as/for people/to meet/one another
3) President Kennedy's/the United States/goal for/a man/was to put/on the moon
4) a lot of/the lost child/ground to/cover in/their search for/The volunteers had
5) Helen felt her/job as his/boss was becoming/relationship with Bill/in her/the main hurdle

WORD ELIMINATION:
Words from this unit are on the left. Five possible synonyms for each word are given below. Only three of the words are true synonyms. Circle the two words that do not belong.

1) staff	a) employees	b) chief	c) personnel	d) officer	e) recruits
2) sociable	a) distant	b) isolated	c) outgoing	d) gregarious	e) congenial
3) goal	a) aim	b) objective	c) beginning	d) aspiration	e) question
4) ground	a) summit	b) soil	c) crease	d) dirt	e) terrain
5) hurdle	a) difficulty	b) jump	c) solution	d) problem	e) barrier

ANSWER KEY:
CIRCLE THE CORRECT MEANING: 1) b 2) c 3) a 4) d 5) e
FILL IN THE BLANKS: 1) sociable 2) hurdle 3) staff 4) goal 5) ground
SYNONYM MATCHING: 1) d 2) c 3) a 4) b 5) e
SENTENCE BUILDING:
1) The company president gave every one of his staff a bonus for a job well done.
2) The dance was designed as a sociable event for people to meet one another.
3) President Kennedy's goal for the United States was to put a man on the moon.
4) The volunteers had a lot of ground to cover in their search for the lost child.
5) Helen felt her job as his boss was becoming the main hurdle in her relationship with Bill.
WORD ELIMINATION:
1) b,d 2) a,b 3) c,e 4) a,c 5) b,c

1) *table* (noun)

Examples:
a)   The subject of today's math class will be the multiplication table.
b)   The periodic table of the elements includes such minerals as gold, zinc and cobalt.
c)   The contents of the book were listed in a table on the second page.

Circle the correct meaning:

a) bench   b) chart   c) plank   d) board   e) divide

2) *trust* (noun)

Examples:
a)   Being honest with your friends is the best way to earn their trust.
b)   Mrs. Karhimi put her trust in the dog because she new it would protect her.
c)   Americans gave George Bush a vote of trust for the way he handled the crisis in New York.

Circle the correct meaning:

a) suspicion   b) wonder   c) doubt   d) confidence   e) misgiving

3) *blank* (adjective)

Examples:
a)   Connie had a blank look on her face and seemed confused about the question.
b)   William took out a blank sheet of paper and began to draw pictures.
c)   Jim found a blank space in the parking lot where his car was supposed to be.

Circle the correct meaning:

a) colorful   b) square   c) smiling   d) complete   e) empty

4) *hilarious* (adjective)

Examples:
a)   Jim Carey did his hilarious impression of Michael Jackson on the Tonight Show.
b)   Paul told a hilarious joke that had everyone buckled over with laughter.
c)   The children enjoyed the hilarious antics of the clown troupe.

Circle the correct meaning:

a) funny   b) unexpected   c) depressing   d) brief   e) accurate

5) *thug* (noun)

Examples:
a)   The couple was robbed by a thug who followed them from the movie theater.
b)   Police warned citizens there was an armed thug roaming their neighborhood at night.
c)   Drake was wearing the same dark jacket worm by the thug who robbed the bank.

Circle the correct meaning:

a) counselor   b) leader   c) hooligan   d) teacher   e) employee

FILL IN THE BLANKS:

Below are five sentences. Each contains a blank. Fill in the blank by using the appropriate word from this unit. Each word is used only once.

1) When I meditate I try to make my mind go ________________.
2) Many people thought Gord was a ________________ because he rode a motorcycle.
3) Shrek is an ________________ comedy about an ogre on a quest to regain his swamp.
4) Marilyn had the ________________ of all the players on her team.
5) A ________________ posted on the wall listed all the times people could swim at the pool.

SYNONYM MATCHING:

On the left are words from this unit. Draw a line to the word on the right with the closest meaning.

1) table	a) amusing
2) trust	b) index
3) blank	c) punk
4) hilarious	d) reliance
5) thug	e) vacant

SENTENCE BUILDING:

Assemble the scrambled clues below to form proper sentences.

1) a table/listed all/assets in/The accountant/the company
2) successful marriage/that trust was/The priest said/to a/the key
3) in his bedroom/the blank wall/to hang on/buy a painting/James wanted to
4) expected such/at an opera/No one/a hilarious/performance
5) Parents demanded/from school/that the principal/young thug/expel the

WORD ELIMINATION:

Words from this unit are on the left. Five possible synonyms for each word are given below. Only three of the words are true synonyms. Circle the two words that do not belong.

1) table	a) volume	b) graph	c) directory	d) design	e) list
2) trust	a) faith	b) belief	c) lie	d) deception	e) assurance
3) blank	a) full	b) packed	c) clean	d) clear	e) unoccupied
4) hilarious	a) comical	b) dull	c) laughable	d) boring	e) humorous
5) thug	a) gangster	b) brute	c) protector	d) ruffian	e) partner

---

ANSWER KEY:

CIRCLE THE CORRECT MEANING: 1) b 2) d 3) e 4) a 5) c
FILL IN THE BLANKS: 1) blank 2) thug 3) hilarious 4) trust 5) table
SYNONYM MATCHING: 1) b 2) d 3) e 4) a 5) c
SENTENCE BUILDING:
1) The accountant listed all the company assets in a table.
2) The priest said that trust was the key to a successful marriage.
3) James wanted to buy a painting to hang on the blank wall in his bedroom.
4) No one expected such a hilarious performance at an opera.
5) Parents demanded that the principal expel the young thug from school.
WORD ELIMINATION:
1) a,d 2) c,d 3) a,b 4) b,d 5) c,e

1) *captain* (noun)

Examples:
a)   The captain of the Titanic went down with the ship.
b)   Dave Keon was a popular captain of the Toronto Maple Leafs during the 1960s.
c)   Melissa was named captain of the high school debating team.

Circle the correct meaning:

a) leader   b) member   c) participant   d) servant   e) worker

2) *devotion* (noun)

Examples:
a)   Father McGregor showed enormous devotion for his job.
b)   Professor Williams felt his students lacked the devotion needed to pass the class.
c)   Joseph's parents were proud of the devotion he had for his piano playing.

Circle the correct meaning:

a) curiosity   b) enthusiasm   c) dislike   d) ignorance   e) innocence

3) *figure* (noun)

Examples:
a)   Bruce questioned the figure he was shown for the cost of his car repairs.
b)   Sports reporters could not believe the figure the Yankees were offering to pay Roger Clemons.
c)   Lawyers could not agree on a figure for the service they provided.

Circle the correct meaning:

a) equal   b) individual   c) resident   d) singular   e) amount

4) *sickly* (adjective)

Examples:
a)   Kelly looked sickly after spending three weeks in the jungle.
b)   Cancer caused George Harrison to become sickly prior to his death.
c)   Nurses made regular house calls to take care of the sickly old woman.

Circle the correct meaning:

a) cheery   b) happy   c) unhealthy   d) nourished   e) strong

5) *roll* (noun)

Examples:
a)   The gambler pulled out a roll of fifty dollar bills.
b)   A roll of copper wire fell off the truck and slammed into the car.
c)   Movers had to lift a roll of carpet onto the back of the truck.

Circle the correct meaning:

a) square   b) triangle   c) fold   d) coil   e) handful

THE VOCABULARY DIET: UNIT 9

FILL IN THE BLANKS:
Below are five sentences. Each contains a blank. Fill in the blank by using the appropriate word from this unit. Each word is used only once.

1) The cows were chewing on a giant ___________________ of hay delivered by the farmer.
2) The ___________________ on the receipt did not match the price on the box.
3) William Shatner played the part of ___________________ Kirk on the television show Star Trek.
4) It takes a lot of ___________________ to properly train a wild animal.
5) The famine had left many children undernourished and looking ___________________.

SYNONYM MATCHING:
On the left are words from this unit. Draw a line to the word on the right with the closest meaning.

1) captain	a) commander
2) devotion	b) reel
3) figure	c) ailing
4) sickly	d) quantity
5) roll	e) zeal

SENTENCE BUILDING:
Assemble the scrambled clues below to form proper sentences.

1) the crew on/was an/The captain of/board the plane/experienced pilot
2) of the department/She was rewarded/promotion to manager/for her devotion/with a/to the job
3) they had/previously discussed/The figure they/much higher than/accepted was
4) The sickly/for tests/dog was taken/animal hospital/to the
5) in the store/A large roll/fell from the/top shelf/of wallpaper

WORD ELIMINATION:
Words from this unit are on the left. Five possible synonyms for each word are given below. Only three of the words are true synonyms. Circle the two words that do not belong.

1) captain	a) servant	b) head	c) slave	d) chief	e) boss
2) devotion	a) keenness	b) eagerness	c) apathy	d) uncaring	e) passion
3) figure	a) piece	b) several	c) total	d) cost	e) sum
4) sickly	a) muscular	b) weak	c) ill	d) unwell	e) brawny
5) roll	a) spool	b) cylinder	c) package	d) tube	e) glass

ANSWER KEY:

CIRCLE THE CORRECT MEANING: 1) a 2) b 3) e 4) c 5) d
FILL IN THE BLANKS: 1) roll 2) figure 3) captain 4) devotion 5) sickly
SYNONYM MATCHING: 1) a 2) e 3) d 4) c 5) b
SENTENCE BUILDING:
1) The captain of the crew on board the plane was an experienced pilot.
2) She was rewarded for her devotion to the job with a promotion to manager of the department.
3) The figure they accepted was much higher than they had previously discussed.
4) The sickly dog was taken to the animal hospital for tests.
5) A large roll of wallpaper fell from the top shelf in the store.
WORD ELIMINATION:
1) a,c 2) c,d 3) a,b 4) a,e 5) c,e

1) *monster* (adjective)

Examples:
a)   After the fight the boxer received treatment for a monster headache.
b)   The gambler walked away with a monster jackpot from the poker game.
c)   For earning such good marks in school Jane received a monster banana split from her dad.

Circle the correct meaning:

a) tiny   b) skinny   c) small   d) huge   e) fearsome

2) *precious* (adjective)

Examples:
a)   The ring was precious to Karen even though it was made of plastic.
b)   Barbara told everyone who would listen that her sons were her most precious possession.
c)   Curtis did not want to waste precious time worrying about the little things in life.

Circle the correct meaning:

a) important   b) useless   c) worthless   d) cheap   e) unexpected

3) *arrogant* (adjective)

Examples:
a)   The girls disliked Cameron because of the arrogant way in which he treated them.
b)   The new boss was arrogant toward employees at the company.
c)   Mrs. Cleaver thought it was arrogant of Eddie not to invited Wally to the birthday party.

Circle the correct meaning:

a) humble   b) egotistical   c) modest   d) meek   e) pleasant

4) *kick* (noun)

Examples:
a)   Devan thought the roller coaster was a real kick.
b)   Maria said she got a kick out of scuba diving in shark-infested water.
c)   Fans got a real kick out of the way Elvis shook his hips.

Circle the correct meaning:

a) sadness   b) grief   c) heartache   d) misery   e) thrill

5) *penalty* (noun)

Examples:
a)   Marion was prepared to suffer the penalty for robbing the bank.
b)   Tie Domi suffered a severe penalty for the errant elbow he threw in the playoffs.
c)   The penalty for driving without car insurance is now $5,000.00.

Circle the correct meaning:

a) reward   b) bonus   c) punishment   d) prize   e) gift

FILL IN THE BLANKS:

Below are five sentences. Each contains a blank. Fill in the blank by using the appropriate word from this unit. Each word is used only once.

1) Many of Bill Clinton's harshest critics felt he was too _________________ to be a good leader.
2) Gladys asked the fireman to save her _________________ kitten from the fire.
3) Sharon got a _________________ out of the way the dog chased its tail.
4) Chopping off a hand was often the _________________ received by thieves in ancient cultures.
5) Wayne Gretzky received a _________________ ovation when he skated onto the ice.

SYNONYM MATCHING:

On the left are words from this unit. Draw a line to the word on the right with the closest meaning.

1)	monster	a)	gigantic
2)	precious	b)	treasured
3)	arrogant	c)	snobbish
4)	kick	d)	joy
5)	penalty	e)	sentence

SENTENCE BUILDING:

Assemble the scrambled clues below to form proper sentences.

1) a monster/the store/There was/waiting to get/line-up outside/in for/the sale.
2) Spending weekends/precious memory/at the cottage/of her childhood/ was Fran's most
3) in the courtroom/impress the judge/Al's arrogant attitude/did not
4) through the carwash/to roller blade/Martin thought/a kick/it would be
5) for dumping toxins/ordered to pay/into the river/The company was/a substantial penalty

WORD ELIMINATION:

Words from this unit are on the left. Five possible synonyms for each word are given below. Only three of the words are true synonyms. Circle the two words that do not belong.

1)	monster	a) enormous	b) sketchy	c) giant	d) petite	e) massive
2)	precious	a) cherished	b) dear	c) apathy	d) uncaring	e) loved
3)	arrogant	a) naive	b) dumb	c) proud	d) vain	e) smug
4)	kick	a) delight	b) exposed	c) pleasure	d) buzz	e) helpless
5)	penalty	a) incentive	b) fine	c) extra	d) reprimand	e) cost

---

ANSWER KEY:

CIRCLE THE CORRECT MEANING: 1) d 2) a 3) b 4) e 5) c
FILL IN THE BLANKS: 1) arrogant 2) precious 3) kick 4) penalty 5) monster
SYNONYM MATCHING: 1) a 2) b 3) c 4) d 5) e
SENTENCE BUILDING:
1) There was a monster line-up outside the store waiting to get in for the sale.
2) Spending weekends at the cottage was Fran's most precious memory of her childhood.
3) Al's arrogant attitude in the courtroom did not impress the judge.
4) Martin thought it would be a kick to roller blade through the carwash.
5) The company was ordered to pay a substantial penalty for dumping toxins into the river.
WORD ELIMINATION:
1) b,d 2) c,d 3) a,b 4) b,e 5) a,c

1) *bound* (adjective)

Examples:
a)   General Montgomery was bound by his duty as commander to lead the troops into battle.
b)   Janice donated blood because she was bound by a sense of responsibility to help others.
c)   Employees were bound by contract not to reveal the details of the settlement.

Circle the correct meaning:

a) compelled   b) freed   c) liberated   d) unchained   e) insecure

2) *chest* (noun)

Examples:
a)   The blankets were stored in an old silver chest down in the basement.
b)   The pirates put the treasure in a wooden chest and buried it in the sand.
c)   The chest contained several hidden drawers full of gold coins.

Circle the correct meaning:

a) bag   b) trunk   c) hole   d) jar   e) bank

3) *broke* (adjective)

Examples:
a)   Doug had been broke since the day he lost his job at the paper mill.
b)   James complained he was broke and could not pay his share of the rent.
c)   Cindy decided to save her money because she did not want to be broke at Christmas.

Circle the correct meaning:

a) rich   b) wealthy   c) successful   d) penniless   e) well-to-do

4) *disappointment* (noun)

Examples:
a)   Suffering a concussion was a major disappointment to hockey player Eric Lindros.
b)   Failure to win a gold medal at the Olympics was a disappointment to athlete.
c)   Loosing her dog grooming business was a disappointment to Carol.

Circle the correct meaning:

a) triumph   b) victory   c) feat   d) success   e) letdown

5) *immense* (adjective)

Examples:
a)   Wrestling has an immense following in North America.
b)   There was an immense feeling of joy within the group after they won the lottery.
c)   The pain in Janet's back was immense after her car accident.

Circle the correct meaning:

a) miniscule   b) little   c) enormous   d) brief   e) short

THE VOCABULARY DIET: UNIT 11

FILL IN THE BLANKS:

Below are five sentences. Each contains a blank. Fill in the blank by using the appropriate word from this unit. Each word is used only once.

1) The lawyer was _________________ by law to keep details of the case confidential.
2) Bruce felt an _________________ sense of relief when he finally found his wallet.
3) A broken handle on the _________________ made it difficult to lift.
4) Years of over-spending had left the city _________________ and unable to pay its staff.
5) Hank quit his job to avoid the _________________ of being fired by his boss.

SYNONYM MATCHING:

On the left are words from this unit. Draw a line to the word on the right with the closest meaning.

1) bound	a) container
2) chest	b) failure
3) broke	c) colossal
4) disappointment	d) required
5) immense	e) cash-strapped

SENTENCE BUILDING:

Assemble the scrambled clues below to form proper sentences.

1) ended the war/were bound by/Both countries/the treaty that
2) by Helen's family/The chest was/heirlooms collected/full of
3) want to admit/father that/to his/Justin did not/he was broke
4) The loss of/and his brothers/disappointment to Domenic/their father was/a great
5) immense pleasure/gave Todd/wife relax/Watching his

WORD ELIMINATION:

Words from this unit are on the left. Five possible synonyms for each word are given below. Only three of the words are true synonyms. Circle the two words that do not belong.

1) bound	a) unable	b) obliged	c) obligated	d) unwilling	e) forced
2) chest	a) box	b) vault	c) safe	d) countertop	e) shelf
3) broke	a) ruined	b) bust	c) investing	d) bankrupt	e) interest
4) disappointment	a) gladness	b) frustration	c) setback	d) thrill	e) defeat
5) immense	a) vast	b) equal	c) similar	d) giant	e) huge

ANSWER KEY:

CIRCLE THE CORRECT MEANING: 1) a 2) b 3) d 4) e 5) c
FILL IN THE BLANKS: 1) bound 2) immense 3) chest 4) broke 5) disappointment
SYNONYM MATCHING: 1) d 2) a 3) e 4) b 5) c
SENTENCE BUILDING:
1) Both countries were bound by the treaty that ended the war.
2) The chest was full of heirlooms collected by Helen's family.
3) Justin did not want to admit to his father that he was broke.
4) The loss of their father was a great disappointment to Domenic and his brothers.
5) Watching his wife relax gave Todd immense pleasure.
WORD ELIMINATION:
1) a,d 2) d,e 3) c,e 4) a,d 5) b,c

1) *hint* (noun)

Examples:
a)   There was a hint of fear in the student's voice as she gave the speech.
b)   The sauce served with the pasta had just a hint of garlic in it.
c)   The forecast called for cloudy skies with a hint of sunshine all day.

Circle the correct meaning:

a) abundance   b) quantity   c) excess   d) trace   e) downpour

2) *cause* (noun)

Examples:
a)   The children could not explain the cause of the mysterious fire.
b)   The cause of the hostilities could be traced back a thousand years.
c)   Doctors examined the x-rays in an attempt to discover the cause of death.

Circle the correct meaning:

a) reason   b) effect   c) temperature   d) date   e) location

3) *malicious* (adjective)

Examples:
a)   Julia Roberts was upset by the malicious comments printed about her in the magazine.
b)   The protestors yelled malicious slogans at United Nations members leaving the conference.
c)   The mayor received dozens of malicious letters from angry residents.

Circle the correct meaning:

a) pleasant   b) complimentary   c) honest   d) loud   e) hateful

4) *remains* (noun)

Examples:
a)   Crows pecked at the remains of the dead raccoon.
b)   Family members were called to the morgue to identify the remains.
c)   Nothing was left of the remains except a pile of dry bones.

Circle the correct meaning:

a) possession   b) carcass   c) items   d) individual   e) spirit

5) *peer* (noun)

Examples:
a)   William remembered Oscar as a peer of his from Harvard University.
b)   Police feared that Tracy was kidnapped by a peer in her office.
c)   Matthew had always considered Bryan a loyal peer in the law firm.

Circle the correct meaning:

a) enemy   b) rival   c) equal   d) foe   e) adversary

THE VOCABULARY DIET: UNIT 12

FILL IN THE BLANKS:

Below are five sentences. Each contains a blank. Fill in the blank by using the appropriate word from this unit. Each word is used only once.

1) Sheila left instructions to ensure her _________________ were scattered across the ocean.
2) Brent had no idea who was spreading such _________________ rumors about him.
3) There was a _________________ of remorse in Misty's voice when she spoke.
4) An electrician was called in to determine the _________________ of the electrical failure.
5) There was not a single _________________ of Dean's who admired his hard work.

SYNONYM MATCHING:

On the left are words from this unit. Draw a line to the word on the right with the closest meaning.

1) hint a) root
2) cause b) dead body
3) malicious c) contemporary
4) remains d) slight amount
5) peer e) spiteful

SENTENCE BUILDING:

Assemble the scrambled clues below to form proper sentences.

1) about Jenson's disappearance/feel a hint/heard the news/He did not/of sorrow/when he
2) collapse of/the building/An architect was/investigate the cause/of the/brought in to
3) Members of/grew tired/speeches full/the union/of hearing/of malicious lies
4) into the grave/lowered slowly/by family members/The remains were
5) from the fire/Mark was identified/as the man/by a peer/the baby/who rescued

WORD ELIMINATION:

Words from this unit are on the left. Five possible synonyms for each word are given below. Only three of the words are true synonyms. Circle the two words that do not belong.

1) hint a) smidgen b) dash c) bounty d) ample e) pinch
2) cause a) foundation b) thanks c) source d) grounds e) treat
3) malicious a) dreamy b) concerned c) mean d) nasty e) cruel
4) remains a) corpse b) spouse c) cadaver d) skeleton e) relative
5) peer a) colleague b) cohort c) competitor d) associate e) customer

---

ANSWER KEY:

CIRCLE THE CORRECT MEANING: 1) d 2) a 3) e 4) b 5) c
FILL IN THE BLANKS: 1) remains 2) malicious 3) hint 4) cause 5) peer
SYNONYM MATCHING: 1) d 2) a 3) e 4) b 5) c
SENTENCE BUILDING:
1) He did not feel a hint of sorrow when he heard the news about Jenson's disappearance.
2) An architect was brought in to investigate the cause of the collapse of the building.
3) Members of the union grew tired of hearing speeches full of malicious lies.
4) The remains were lowered slowly into the grave by family members.
5) Mark was identified by a peer as the man who rescued the baby from the fire.
WORD ELIMINATION:
1) c,d 2) b,e 3) a,b 4) b,e 5) c,e

1) *feature* (noun)

Examples:
a)   Pinocchio's most prominent feature was a wooden nose that grew each time he told a lie.
b)   The most popular feature of the Corvette was its powerful high-performance engine.
c)   A backyard swimming pool was a standard feature of homes in the neighborhood.

Circle the correct meaning:

a) default   b) defect   c) characteristic   d) problem   e) expense

2) *essential* (adjective)

Examples:
a)   Vitamins are essential to a balanced diet.
b)   Hospitals and police departments are considered essential services of any modern city.
c)   For a democracy to work properly it is essential that every citizen be allowed to vote.

Circle the correct meaning:

a) necessary   b) ignorant   c) disown   d) popular   e) edible

3) *clasp* (noun)

Examples:
a)   Bills pants fell down when the clasp broke off his belt.
b)   Roger nearly plunged to the ground when the clasp on his parachute loosened.
c)   The clasp holding Wayne's boot together was made of solid gold.

Circle the correct meaning:

a) leather   b) fastener   c) string   d) plug   e) repair

4) *pal* (noun)

Examples:
a)   Rob was the one pal Dave could always count on when he needed help.
b)   Conrad had a pal in Thailand that always sent him a gift for Christmas.
c)   Maddy's best pal was her dog Jake.

Circle the correct meaning:

a) adversary   b) enemy   c) conquest   d) relative   e) friend

5) *mishap* (noun)

Examples:
a)   An investigation proved the airline crash was simply an unfortunate mishap.
b)   Organizers took every precaution to ensure no mishap would occur during the performance.
c)   The mishap caused serious injury to twelve people.

Circle the correct meaning:

a) celebration   b) mystery   c) surprise   d) accident   e) plan

FILL IN THE BLANKS:

Below are five sentences. Each contains a blank. Fill in the blank by using the appropriate word from this unit. Each word is used only once.

1) Jeff was surprised his _________________ made the long trip from Vancouver to visit him.
2) The shuttle's most unique design _________________ was its robot arm.
3) Witnesses said the _________________ was the result of a faulty traffic light.
4) Doctors warned Mr. Teeple that surgery was _________________ to eliminate the disease.
5) The door of the tent was kept open by a _________________ on the canvas.

SYNONYM MATCHING:

On the left are words from this unit. Draw a line to the word on the right with the closest meaning.

1) feature   a) hook
2) essential   b) misfortune
3) clasp   c) attribute
4) pal   d) buddy
5) mishap   e) vital

SENTENCE BUILDING:

Assemble the scrambled clues below to form proper sentences.

1) John loosened/on his pants/the clasp/after eating dessert
2) of the company/to the well-being/the workforce/It was essential/to downsize
3) The main feature/wooden roller coaster/of the amusement/a large/park was
4) physical health/in such poor/see his pal/Darren was/sad to
5) in to/of the mishap/Experts were called/investigate the cause

WORD ELIMINATION:

Words from this unit are on the left. Five possible synonyms for each word are given below. Only three of the words are true synonyms. Circle the two words that do not belong.

1) feature	a) injury	b) primary	c) trait	d) quality	e) aspect
2) essential	a) important	b) overlooked	c) crucial	d) ignored	e) critical
3) clasp	a) opening	b) clip	c) catch	d) snap	e) applause
4) pal	a) mate	b) chum	c) admirer	d) stalker	e) companion
5) mishap	a) catastrophe	b) fate	c) shape	d) calamity	e) disaster

1) *advice* (noun)

Examples:
a)   She decided to follow the advice of her doctor and check herself into the hospital.
b)   Madeline respected the advice she was given by her mother.
c)   Mrs. Beasby was always offering her neighbors advice they didn't want.

Circle the correct meaning:

a) compliments   b) suggestion   c) presents   d) payment   e) recipe

2) *junk* (noun)

Examples:
a)   The yard was littered with junk left by the previous owners.
b)   During the strike by sanitation workers junk began to pile up on city streets.
c)   "You will not be allowed to go out until you clean the junk from your room," said Mark's mother.

Circle the correct meaning:

a) jewelry   b) candy   c) furniture   d) rubbish   e) valuables

3) *mammoth* (adjective)

Examples:
a)   The mining company had dug a mammoth hole in the side of the mountain.
b)   The bus was carrying a group of mammoth football players.
c)   The accident on the bridge caused a mammoth traffic jam.

Circle the correct meaning:

a) minor   b) insignificant   c) wonderful   d) short   e) enormous

4) *graphic* (adjective)

Examples:
a)   The story described the battle in graphic details.
b)   The subject matter of the movie was too graphic to show to children.
c)   Father McPhee was not impressed with the graphic language being used in church.

Circle the correct meaning:

a) detailed   b) vague   c) confusing   d) humorous   e) dull

5) *fragment* (noun)

Examples:
a)   Doctors removed a fragment of the bullet from the victim's shoulder.
b)   The dog had a fragment of broken glass stuck in his paw.
c)   A large fragment of the jet liner was recovered from the ocean floor.

Circle the correct meaning:

a) mend   b) repair   c) piece   d) dissolve   e) soften

THE VOCABULARY DIET: UNIT 14

FILL IN THE BLANKS:

Below are five sentences. Each contains a blank. Fill in the blank by using the appropriate word from this unit. Each word is used only once.

1) Truckloads of _________________ were being hauled from the construction site.
2) Crime scene photos were so _________________ the local newspaper would not print them.
3) Even a tiny _________________ of dust could spoil the experiment.
4) A _________________ snowdrift had blocked the entrance to the barn.
5) Janice was a troubled youth in need of some good _______________.

SYNONYM MATCHING:

On the left are words from this unit. Draw a line to the word on the right with the closest meaning.

1) advice   a) bit
2) junk   b) colossal
3) mammoth   c) litter
4) graphic   d) realistic
5) fragment   e) recommendation

SENTENCE BUILDING:

Assemble the scrambled clues below to form proper sentences.

1) to provide/The counselor's/career advice/job was/students with
2) A yard sale/way to sell/around the house/old junk found/is a good
3) destroyed by a/the fuel tank/The shuttle was/mammoth explosion in
4) Graphic scenes/it unbearable/of violence in/to watch/the movie made
5) of the government/A large fragment/of the/supported the policy/population still

WORD ELIMINATION:

Words from this unit are on the left. Five possible synonyms for each word are given below. Only three of the words are true synonyms. Circle the two words that do not belong.

1) advice	a) invoice	b) counsel	c) language	d) suggestion	e) guidance
2) junk	a) scrap	b) treasure	c) garbage	d) wealth	e) trash
3) mammoth	a) oval	b) massive	c) massive	d) immense	e) hairy
4) graphic	a) rural	b) explicit	c) vivid	d) simple	e) lifelike
5) fragment	a) portion	b) entire	c) complete	d) part	e) section

ANSWER KEY:

CIRCLE THE CORRECT MEANING: 1) b 2) d 3) e 4) a 5) c
FILL IN THE BLANKS: 1) junk 2) graphic 3) fragment 4) mammoth 5) advice
SYNONYM MATCHING: 1) e 2) c 3) b 4) d 5) a
SENTENCE BUILDING:
1) The counselor's job was to provide students with career advice.
2) A yard sale is a good way to sell old junk found around the house.
3) The shuttle was destroyed by a mammoth explosion in the fuel tank.
4) Graphic scenes of violence in the movie made it unbearable to watch.
5) A large fragment of the population still supported the policy of the government.
WORD ELIMINATION:
1) a,c 2) b,d 3) a,e 4) a,d 5) b,c

1) *absurd* (adjective)

Examples:
a)   Air travel seemed like an absurd concept to people of the 19th century.
b)   The New York Yankees paid an absurd amount of money to acquire their latest player.
c)   Some of the greatest success stories began with an absurd idea.

Circle the correct meaning:

a) regular   b) believable   c) agreeable   d) ridiculous   e) acceptable

2) *cruel* (adjective)

Examples:
a)   Activists condemned the zoo for being cruel to the animals in its care.
b)   Stephen was hurt by the cruel comments made by his brother.
c)   The country was run by a cruel dictator who often tortured political prisoners.

Circle the correct meaning:

a) thankful   b) unkind   c) pleasing   d) friendly   d) crunchy

3) *fabulous* (adjective)

Examples:
a)   The trip to Paris included a fabulous tour of the Eiffel Tower.
b)   Marilyn looked fabulous in a white dress and matching pearl necklace.
c)   The play received fabulous reviews from everyone lucky enough to have had a ticket.

Circle the correct meaning:

a) itchy   b) tiny   c) furry   d) questionable   e) wonderful

4) *grime* (noun)

Examples:
a)   The sidewalks were covered with grime caused by the local steel factory.
b)   It took six hours to scrub the grime off the kitchen floor.
c)   The dentist was shocked by the grime on her patient's teeth.

Circle the correct meaning:

a) filth   b) shine   c) color   d) reflection   e) odor

5) *wallop* (noun)

Examples:
a)   The boxer collapsed from the force of the wallop to his head.
b)   The storm continued to wallop houses on the island.
c)   The unexpected wallop threw the hockey player off balance.

Circle the correct meaning:

a) stroke   b) caress   c) whack   d) tickle   e) carry

FILL IN THE BLANKS:

Below are five sentences. Each contains a blank. Fill in the blank by using the appropriate word from this unit. Each word is used only once.

1) The car took an enormous _________________ when hit by the truck.
2) A _________________ collection of ancient pottery was on display at the museum.
3) The cleaning company used chemicals to strip the _________________ from the church walls.
4) Alison thought the prank phone call was a _________________ joke to play on an old woman.
5) Jim was starring in an _________________ comedy about a man who gets turned into a dog.

SYNONYM MATCHING:

On the left are words from this unit. Draw a line to the word on the right with the closest meaning.

1) absurd   a) grunge
2) cruel   b) smack
3) fabulous   c) tremendous
4) grime   d) foolish
5) wallop   e) nasty

SENTENCE BUILDING:

Assemble the scrambled clues below to form proper sentences.

1) raw eggs/His wife/for eating/was absurd/thought he
2) him to bed/to the dog/for being cruel/Kirk's mother sent
3) Elizabeth looked/coming back/from her vacation/fabulous after
4) the bathroom/The hotel guests/the grime in/were disgusted by
5) an enormous/Bradley received/into the tree/he ran/wallop when

WORD ELIMINATION:

Words from this unit are on the left. Five possible synonyms for each word are given below. Only three of the words are true synonyms. Circle the two words that do not belong.

1) absurd	a) silly	b) righteous	c) ludicrous	d) considerable	e) stupid
2) cruel	a) caring	b) category	c) malicious	d) mean	e) brutal
3) fabulous	a) magnificent	b) marvelous	c) ugly	d) great	e) quiet
4) grime	a) fragrance	b) scum	c) slime	d) dirt	e) flavor
5) wallop	a) bash	b) belt	c) touch	d) melt	e) hit

ANSWER KEY:

CIRCLE THE CORRECT MEANING: 1) d 2) b 3) e 4) a 5) c
FILL IN THE BLANKS: 1) wallop 2) fabulous 3) grime 4) cruel 5) absurd
SYNONYM MATCHING: 1) d 2) e 3) c 4) a 5) b
SENTENCE BUILDING:
1) His wife thought he was absurd for eating raw eggs.
2) Kirk's mother sent him to bed for being cruel to the dog.
3) Elizabeth looked fabulous after coming back from her vacation.
4) The hotel guests were disgusted by the grime in the bathroom.
5) Bradley received an enormous wallop when he ran into the tree.
WORD ELIMINATION:
1) b,d 2) a,b 3) c,e 4) a,e 5) c,d

1) *chaperone* (noun)

Examples:
a)   Nancy's dad was asked to serve as chaperone at the high school dance.
b)   She hired a chaperone to ensure her protection.
c)   Sister Margaret insisted all the nuns be accompanied by a chaperone when visiting the war zone.

Circle the correct meaning:

a) slave   b) guardian   c) teacher   d) employee   e) mayor

2) *employer* (noun)

Examples:
a)   Tammi was between jobs and searching for a new employer.
b)   Her previous employer said she was a very hard-working individual.
c)   The economy was slow and it was very difficult to find an employer that paid good wages.

Circle the correct meaning:

a) company   b) money   c) wages   d) debts   e) duty

3) *freakish* (adjective)

Examples:
a)   A spokesperson for the group could not explain their freakish behavior.
b)   Alice Cooper was a rock musician with a freakish on-stage persona.
c)   Friends were shocked at Alison's freakish hairstyle.   .

Circle the correct meaning:

a) cuddly   b) predictable   c) exciting   d) bizarre   e) vuluptuous

4) *hunger* (noun)

Examples:
a)   He developed his hunger to play professional football at an early age.
b)   His hunger for excitement was the main reason he was going rock climbing.
c)   Jackie said she had a strong hunger for chicken wings.

Circle the correct meaning:

a) discussion   b) slumber   c) require   d) obtain   e) desire

5) *pedigree* (noun)

Examples:
a)   Her pedigree could be traced back several centuries.
b)   With his quaint English charm there was no doubt about his pedigree.
c)   The Golden Retriever's remarkable pedigree included a father that was national champion.

Circle the correct meaning:

a) temperature   b) circuit   c) ancestry   d) geography   e) smile

FILL IN THE BLANKS:
Below are five sentences. Each contains a blank. Fill in the blank by using the appropriate word from this unit. Each word is used only once.

1) The Backstreet Boys always traveled with a _________________ to watch over them.
2) You could see the _________________ in the athlete's eyes as she crossed the finish line.
3) The clown was hurt in a _________________ accident after his clown suit caught fire.
4) Mrs. Sullivan's _________________ called seeking a reference for a new applicant.
5) Breeders were impressed by the horse's _________________.

SYNONYM MATCHING:
On the left are words from this unit. Draw a line to the word on the right with the closest meaning.

1) chaperone   a) bodyguard
2) employer   b) passion
3) freakish   c) business
4) hunger   d) abnormal
5) pedigree   e) bloodline

SENTENCE BUILDING:
Assemble the scrambled clues below to form proper sentences.

1) polite young/was a/college professor/Emily's chaperone
2) Michael/being a/had a/reputation for/generous employer
3) with the ladies/His freakish/not diminish/his popularity/appearance did
4) in business/to a career/lead him/for success/His hunger
5) She was/impeccable pedigree/accepted by/strength of her/the university/on the

WORD ELIMINATION:
Words from this unit are on the left. Five possible synonyms for each word are given below. Only three of the words are true synonyms. Circle the two words that do not belong.

1) chaperone	a) parent	b) supervisor	c) relative	d) escort	e) companion
2) employer	a) foreman	b) director	c) manager	d) option	e) contract
3) freakish	a) unusual	b) approved	c) popular	d) weird	e) strange
4) hunger	a) need	b) flaw	c) yearning	d) digest	e) longing
5) pedigree	a) heritage	b) award	c) origin	d) honor	e) heredity

---

ANSWER KEY:
CIRCLE THE CORRECT MEANING: 1) b 2) a 3) d 4) e 5) c
FILL IN THE BLANKS: 1) chaperone 2) lather 3) freakish 4) employer 5) pedigree
SYNONYM MATCHING: 1) a 2) c 3) d 4) b 5) e
SENTENCE BUILDING:
1) Emily's chaperone was a polite young college professor.
2) Michael had a reputation for being a generous employer.
3) His freakish appearance did not diminish his popularity with the ladies.
4) His hunger for success lead him to a career in business.
5) She was accepted by the university on the strength of her impeccable pedigree.
WORD ELIMINATION:
1) a,c 2) d,e 3) b,c 4) c,e 5) b,d

1) *mockery* (noun)

Examples:
a) Jimmy's foolish behavior made a mockery of the award ceremony.
b) Mrs. Beamer felt the children's poorly written essays were a mockery of education.
c) The whole purpose of the article was to expose the mockery of government policy.

Circle the correct meaning:

a) apology   b) forgiveness   c) chirping   d) adventure   e) travesty

2) *chintzy* (adjective)

Examples:
a) Vendors at the flea market were known for selling chintzy merchandise.
b) A tight leather mini skirt was part of the chintzy outfit Bonnie wore to the dance.
c) The chintzy decorations included neon signs and velvet-covered walls.

Circle the correct meaning:

a) trashy   b) understated   c) regal   d) valuable   e) exclusive

3) *counterfeit* (adjective)

Examples:
a) The merchandise had been purchased with counterfeit money.
b) Counterfeit copies of Disney movies were being sold at the video store.
c) The terrorists had used counterfeit documents to cross the border.

Circle the correct meaning:

a) costly   b) fake   c) purchased   d) curious   e) heavy

4) *vow* (noun)

Examples:
a) He made a vow to his wife that he would quit smoking.
b) Police were sworn to uphold the law, and Officer Marino respected that vow.
c) Marcy was mad at Michael for breaking his vow of silence about their relationship.

Circle the correct meaning:

a) question   b) speech   c) promise   d) motion   e) gesture

5) *wandering* (adjective)

Examples:
a) Colleen was on the lookout for shoplifters with wandering hands.
b) Mick had a wandering spirit and liked to travel to foreign lands.
c) Harvey had a wandering imagination and could not stay focused in the classroom.

Circle the correct meaning:

a) fixed   b) stagnant   c) effortless   d) roaming   e) sleepy

THE VOCABULARY DIET: UNIT 17

FILL IN THE BLANKS:

Below are five sentences. Each contains a blank. Fill in the blank by using the appropriate word from this unit. Each word is used only once.

1) Mr. Delbert made good on the _________________ he made to buy his son a bicycle.
2) Tommy developed _______________ eyes when he visited the beach.
3) National Lampoon magazine was intended to be a _________________ of the establishment.
4) Stores were selling _______________ souvenirs during the Pope's visit to America.
5) Customs officials had confiscated a shipment of _______________ Rolex watches.

SYNONYM MATCHING:

On the left are words from this unit. Draw a line to the word on the right with the closest meaning.

1) mockery   a) laughingstock
2) chintzy   b) meandering
3) counterfeit   c) declaration
4) vow   d) forged
5) wandering   e) tawdry

SENTENCE BUILDING:

Assemble the scrambled clues below to form proper sentences.

1) court battle/another lengthy/Mr. Tripp was/the mockery of/determined to avoid
2) Guests at the/chintzy decorations/surprised by the/on the walls/governor's mansion were
3) at the event/seized by security/concert tickets were/The counterfeit
4) taken a sacred/the principles of/The priest had/the church/vow to uphold
5) Jim liked to/in the forest/with a compass/go wandering around

WORD ELIMINATION:

Words from this unit are on the left. Five possible synonyms for each word are given below. Only three of the words are true synonyms. Circle the two words that do not belong.

1) mockery	a) supportive	b) helpful	c) charade	d) farce	e) sham
2) chintzy	a) priceless	b) tacky	c) shoddy	d) inferior	e) wealthy
3) counterfeit	a) phoney	b) approved	c) popular	d) bogus	e) imitation
4) vow	a) agreement	b) oath	c) lie	d) fabricate	e) pledge
5) wandering	a) rambling	b) aimless	c) roundabout	d) exact	e) direct

ANSWER KEY:

CIRCLE THE CORRECT MEANING: 1) e 2) a 3) b 4) c 5) d
FILL IN THE BLANKS: 1) vow 2) wandering 3) mockery 4) chintzy 5) counterfeit
SYNONYM MATCHING: 1) a 2) e 3) d 4) c 5) b
SENTENCE BUILDING:
1) Mr. Tripp was determined to avoid the mockery of another lengthy court battle.
2) Guests at the governor's mansion were surprised by the chintzy decorations on the walls.
3) The counterfeit concert tickets were seized by security at the event.
4) The priest had taken a sacred vow to uphold the principles of the church.
5) Jim liked to go wandering around in the forest with a compass.
WORD ELIMINATION:
1) a,b 2) a,e 3) b,c 4) c,d 5) d,e

1) *breezy* (adjective)

Examples:
a)   Strong winds were causing breezy conditions at the airport.
b)   The weather forecast was calling for a warm and breezy afternoon.
c)   The children needed some breezy weather in order to fly their kite.

Circle the correct meaning:

a) still   b) cold   c) windy   d) rainy   e) sunny

2) *cell* (noun)

Examples:
a)   The leader of the demonstration was placed in a private cell for his own protection.
b)   The jail cell was cold and dark.
c)   He had spent most of his adult life locked in a cell.

Circle the correct meaning:

a) bed   b) lockup   c) hotel   d) suite   e) struggle

3) *hardship* (noun)

Examples:
a)   Anthony's children did not understand the hardship he had suffered during the Depression.
b)   Workers faced a long period of hardship after the local factory closed its doors.
c)   The players grew together as a team during the hardship of their first season in the league.

Circle the correct meaning:

a) adversity   b) fun   c) enjoyment   d) ease   e) simplicity

4) *decoration* (noun)

Examples:
a)   He returned from the war with a decoration for courage in battle.
b)   Mary's commander honored her with a decoration for loyal service.
c)   The President was on hand to award a special decoration to the state's best student.

Circle the correct meaning:

a) painting   b) bangle   c) suggestion   d) medal   e) compliment

5) *poise* (noun)

Examples:
a)   The Queen showed great poise during the funeral of Princess Diana.
b)   The pageant contestants were judged on poise as well as beauty.
c)   Steve Yzerman is a hockey player who displays great poise both on and off the ice.

Circle the correct meaning:

a) smile   b) elevation   c) humor   d) intelligence   e) composure

FILL IN THE BLANKS:
Below are five sentences. Each contains a blank. Fill in the blank by using the appropriate word from this unit. Each word is used only once.

1) General McArthur accepted his latest ______________________ on behalf of his soldiers.
2) Great ______________________ is needed to be a successful public speaker.
3) ______________________ conditions on the lake made it unsafe for canoeing.
4) The thought of spending life in a prison ______________________ frightened Jeremy.
5) Janice did not have the strength to endure another year of ______________________.

SYNONYM MATCHING:
On the left are words from this unit. Draw a line to the word on the right with the closest meaning.

1) breezy   a) difficulty
2) cell   b) gusty
3) hardship   c) self-assurance
4) decoration   d) cage
5) poise   e) honor

SENTENCE BUILDING:
Assemble the scrambled clues below to form proper sentences.

1) The country had/its current king/endured years of/the rule of/hardship under
2) was caused by/a high pressure/The breezy weather/the lake/system over
3) effective leader/He lacked/to be an/the poise needed
4) combat soldiers/highest honor/is the/awarded to/The decoration
5) prisoners in a/hold only four/There were eight/cell designed to

WORD ELIMINATION:
Words from this unit are on the left. Five possible synonyms for each word are given below. Only three of the words are true synonyms. Circle the two words that do not belong.

1) breezy   a) freezing   b) blustery   c) scorching   d) blowy   e) brisk
2) cell   a) chamber   b) dungeon   c) pen   d) lobby   e) loft
3) hardship   a) burden   b) joy   c) misfortune   d) affliction e) celebration
4) decoration   a) accolade   b) blame   c) fault   d) badge   e) citation
5) poise   a) rudeness   b) dignity   c) diplomacy   d) anger   e) elegance

---

ANSWER KEY:
CIRCLE THE CORRECT MEANING: 1) c 2) b 3) a 4) d 5) e
FILL IN THE BLANKS: 1) decoration 2) poise 3) breezy 4) cell 5) hardship
SYNONYM MATCHING: 1) b 2) d 3) a 4) e 5) c
SENTENCE BUILDING:
1) The country had endured years of hardship under the rule of its current king.
2) The breezy weather was caused by a high pressure system over the lake.
3) He lacked the poise needed to be an effective leader.
4) The decoration is the highest honor awarded to combat soldiers.
5) There were eight prisoners in a cell designed to hold only four.
WORD ELIMINATION:
1) a,c 2) d,e 3) b,e 4) b,c 5) a,d

1) *beaming* (adjective)

Examples:
a)   Jason was beaming after scoring his first goal in the playoffs.
b)   Cassie's parents were beaming with pride when she graduated from grade school.
c)   Colleen's beaming smile was her most recognizable feature.

Circle the correct meaning:

a) glowing   b) sullen   c) dowdy   d) morose   e) distant

2) *clutter* (noun)

Examples:
a)   The girls were ordered to clean up the clutter in their rooms.
b)   The clutter in the basement was rapidly becoming a fire hazard.
c)   The clutter on his desk was the result of a heavy workload.

Circle the correct meaning:

a) order   b) mess   c) space   d) room   e) variety

3) *dab* (noun)

Examples:
a)   A dab of the blood found at the crime scene was all that was needed to convict the accused.
b)   A dab of moisturizer on her skin was all that Kelly needed to sooth her sunburn.
c)   Directions on the glue bottle indicated only a small dab of glue was needed.

Circle the correct meaning:

a) flood   b) layer   c) bit   d) ton   e) glass

4) *jerk* (noun)

Examples:
a)   Everyone at the party felt Gord was a jerk for eating all the food.
b)   The man in the front row of the movie theater was acting like a jerk by talking during the movie.
c)   Rick admitted he was the jerk who spray-painted the side of the school.

Circle the correct meaning:

a) artist   b) hero   c) individual   d) fool   e) idol

5) *potent* (adjective)

Examples:
a)   Teemu Selane and Paul Kariya were a potent combination when playing hockey together.
b)   Aspirin offers potent relief from a common headache.
c)   Exercise can be a potent form of stress relief.

Circle the correct meaning:

a) weak   b) frail   c) awful   d) miniscule   e) powerful

THE VOCABULARY DIET: UNIT 19

FILL IN THE BLANKS:

Below are five sentences. Each contains a blank. Fill in the blank by using the appropriate word from this unit. Each word is used only once.

1) Mike Tyson often acted like a _____________________ inside and outside the boxing ring.
2) Solar power is a _________________ source of energy.
3) June's father would not allow her to wear even a _______________ of make-up.
4) The department store manager complained about _________________ in the aisles.
5) The actress had a _________________ look on her face when she accepted her Oscar award.

SYNONYM MATCHING:

On the left are words from this unit. Draw a line to the word on the right with the closest meaning.

1) beaming   a) glowing
2) clutter   b) dash
3) dab   c) forceful
4) jerk   d) idiot
5) potent   e) disorder

SENTENCE BUILDING:

Assemble the scrambled clues below to form proper sentences.

1) gave a beaming/the gold medal/The figure skater/performance to capture
2) when mixed together/Ammonia and bleach/produce potent fumes
3) of butter/Adding a dab/to toast/is a great/give it/extra flavor
4) Police were/the Christmas display/who ruined/identify the jerk/trying to
5) her life of/away to charity/Barb decided/to rid/clutter by/giving everything

WORD ELIMINATION:

Words from this unit are on the left. Five possible synonyms for each word are given below. Only three of the words are true synonyms. Circle the two words that do not belong.

1) beaming   a) animated   b) morose   c) radiant   d) surly   e) grinning
2) clutter   a) untidiness b) disarray   c) organized   d) alter   e) muddle
3) dab   a) fleck   b) speck   c) blob   d) punch   e) smack
4) jerk   a) savior   b) legend   c) dope   d) creep   e) twit
5) potent   a) strong   b) feeble   c) fragile   d) mighty   e) forceful

ANSWER KEY:

CIRCLE THE CORRECT MEANING: 1) a 2) b 3) c 4) d 5) e
FILL IN THE BLANKS: 1) jerk 2) potent 3) dab 4) clutter 5) beaming
SYNONYM MATCHING: 1) a 2) e 3) b 4) d 5) c
SENTENCE BUILDING:
1) The figure skater gave a beaming performance to capture the gold medal.
2) Ammonia and bleach produce potent fumes when mixed together.
3) Adding a dab of butter to toast is a great way to give it extra flavor.
4) Police were trying to identify the jerk who ruined the Christmas display.
5) Barb decided to rid her life of clutter by giving everything away to charity.
WORD ELIMINATION:
1) b,d 2) c,d 3) d,e 4) a,b 5) b,c

1) *calamity* (noun)

Examples:
a)   Experts determined the cause of the calamity was a broken rail line.
b)   The most recent calamity on the ski lift caused the death of three people.
c)   Officials hoped to avoid another calamity by banning English soccer fans from the stadium.

Circle the correct meaning:

a) discovery   b) celebration   c) demonstration   d) item   e) disaster

2) *delicate* (adjective)

Examples:
a)   The pottery was too delicate to be moved from the excavation site.
b)   Mrs. Donaldson was in delicate condition after her heart surgery.
c)   Monica's dress was so delicate she was afraid to wash it.

Circle the correct meaning:

a) fragile   b) aggressive   c) immediate   d) unusual   e) strong

3) *flabby* (adjective)

Examples:
a)   Zookeepers scrubbed the elephant's flabby skin with a bristle brush.
b)   The baby's flabby cheeks made her look funny when she smiled.
c)   Her oversized clothes looked flabby on her tiny body.

Circle the correct meaning:

a) taut   b) athletic   c) fit   d) sagging   e) snug

4) *immune* (adjective)

Examples:
a)   Muhammad had grown immune to the insults of his classmates.
b)   Belinda was immune to the problems happening in the office beside hers.
c)   The cement blocks were immune to the effects of the flood waters.

Circle the correct meaning:

a) fond   b) resistant   c) thankful   d) attracted   c) susceptible

5) *noble* (adjective)

Examples:
a)   Offering his seat to the old woman on the bus was a noble thing for Levon to do.
b)   Preston had always tried to conduct himself in a noble fashion.
c)   James Stewart was considered a noble man by Hollywood standards.

Circle the correct meaning:

a) hated   b) confrontational   c) gracious   d) quiet   e) selfish

FILL IN THE BLANKS:
Below are five sentences. Each contains a blank. Fill in the blank by using the appropriate word from this unit. Each word is used only once.

1) Mark had received so many injuries he was now _________________ to the pain.
2) A lack of exercise had caused the dog to grow _________________.
3) The tragic fire that destroyed their barn was the latest _________________ at the family farm.
4) The newborn baby was very _________________ and had to be carefully held.
5) Jane did the _________________ thing and apologized to her sister for ruining her dress.

SYNONYM MATCHING:
On the left are words from this unit. Draw a line to the word on the right with the closest meaning.

1) calamity   a) dignified
2) delicate   b) frail
3) flabby   c) misfortune
4) immune   d) drooping
5) noble   e) protected

SENTENCE BUILDING:
Assemble the scrambled clues below to form proper sentences.

1) Experts predicted a/the nuclear plant/eventually occur at/major calamity would
2) special care/The rose/that requires/delicate flower/is a
3) the champ had/and flabby/Witnesses said/grown slow
4) Sled dogs/to the severe/the Arctic/are immune/winter weather in
5) her money to/to donate all/The millionaire wanted/a noble cause.

WORD ELIMINATION:
Words from this unit are on the left. Five possible synonyms for each word are given below. Only three of the words are true synonyms. Circle the two words that do not belong.

1) calamity	a) closure	b) mishap	c) catastrophe	d) crash	e) tragedy
2) delicate	a) manly	b) burly	c) fragile	d) frail	e) brittle
3) flabby	a) baggy	b) loose	c) slack	d) agile	e) physical
4) immune	a) exempt	b) safe	c) blamed	d) excused	e) contagious
5) noble	a) aristocratic	b) talkative	c) decent	d) thankful	e) righteous

---

ANSWER KEY:
CIRCLE THE CORRECT MEANING: 1) e 2) a 3) d 4) b 5) c
FILL IN THE BLANKS: 1) immune 2) flabby 3) calamity 4) delicate 5) noble
SYNONYM MATCHING: 1) c 2) b 3) d 4) e 5) a
SENTENCE BUILDING:
1) Experts predicted a major calamity would eventually occur at the nuclear plant.
2) The rose is a delicate flower that requires special care.
3) Witnesses said the champ had grown slow and flabby.
4) Sled dogs are immune to the severe winter weather in the Arctic.
5) The millionaire wanted to donate all her money to a noble cause.
WORD ELIMINATION:
1) a,d 2) a,b 3) d,e 4) c,e 5) b,d

1) *joke* (noun)

Examples:
a)   Kristen was the victim of a joke played on her by the local radio station.
b)   Martha realized the policeman at her door was part of an elaborate joke planned by her sister.
c)   All of Linda's friends were in on the joke.

Circle the correct meaning:

a) injury   b) hoax   c) drama   d) travesty   e) question

2) *iron* (adjective)

Examples:
a)   Joseph Stalin ruled the Soviet Union with an iron fist.
b)   The dictator had an iron will and would not tolerate civil disobedience.
c)   The iron might of the army was no match for the ill-equipped peasants.

Circle the correct meaning:

a) firm   b) weak   c) brittle   d) soft   e) wavering

3) *kudos* (noun)

Examples:
a)   The kudos Michael Jordan received for playing basketball were well deserved.
b)   Shelly did not expect such kudos from her new boss.
c)   Kudos rained down for Tom Cruise after his latest acting performance.

Circle the correct meaning:

a) criticism   b) jeers   c) suggestions   d) payment   e) praise

4) *lurid* (adjective)

Examples:
a)   Lurid details of the killer's latest crime were printed in the newspaper.
b)   The magazine was known for printing lurid pictures of female celebrities.
c)   The patient complained he was having lurid dreams about his coworkers.

Circle the correct meaning:

a) tame   b) simple   c) popular   d) graphic   e) impressive

5) *piddling* (adjective)

Examples:
a)   The bank did not bother chasing debtors who owed piddling amounts of money.
b)   Samantha found it hard to live on the piddling wages she earned at the grocery store.
c)   Maria was shocked by the piddling inheritance she was awarded in her mother's will.

Circle the correct meaning:

a) enormous   b) respectful   c) small   d) gigantic   e) substantial

THE VOCABULARY DIET: UNIT 21

FILL IN THE BLANKS:
Below are five sentences. Each contains a blank. Fill in the blank by using the appropriate word from this unit. Each word is used only once.

1) Cassandra was surprised by her boyfriend's _________________ remarks about her mother.
2) Players on the team respected the coach for his _________________ resolve to win.
3) Heather did not want to participate in the practical _________________ being played on Bill.
4) Cheryl's fiancé wanted to discuss the _________________ details of their wedding.
5) The Prime Minster received _________________ from his parliament for doing a good job.

SYNONYM MATCHING:
On the left are words from this unit. Draw a line to the word on the right with the closest meaning.

1) joke   a) prank
2) iron   b) measly
3) kudos   c) strong
4) lurid   d) explicit
5) piddling   e) raves

SENTENCE BUILDING:
Assemble the scrambled clues below to form proper sentences.

1) got hurt/when Sharon accidentally/The joke/backfired
2) of the rebel/throughout the country/The iron methods/leader were feared
3) continued to/come in/The kudos/his death/for Elvis Presley/long after
4) on campus/Heather changed/after witnessing/schools/lurid behavior
5) auto race after/of rain fell/They stopped the/a piddling amount/on the track

WORD ELIMINATION:
Words from this unit are on the left. Five possible synonyms for each word are given below. Only three of the words are true synonyms. Circle the two words that do not belong.

1) joke	a) trick	b) crime	c) cartoon	d) stunt	e) ruse
2) iron	a) gentle	b) caring	c) mighty	d) harsh	e) unyielding
3) kudos	a) acclaim	b) credit	c) flattery	d) blame	e) accusations
4) lurid	a) shocking	b) startling	c) obvious	d) extreme	e) popular
5) piddling	a) enormous	b) puny	c) regular	d) paltry	e) trivial

ANSWER KEY:
CIRCLE THE CORRECT MEANING: 1) b 2) a 3) e 4) d 5) c
FILL IN THE BLANKS: 1) lurid 2) iron 3) joke 4) piddling 5) kudos
SYNONYM MATCHING: 1) a 2) c 3) e 4) d 5) b
SENTENCE BUILDING:
1) The joke backfired when Sharon accidentally got hurt.
2) The iron methods of the rebel leader were feared throughout the country.
3) The kudos for Elvis Presley continued to come in long after his death.
4) Heather changed schools after witnessing lurid behavior on campus.
5) They stopped the auto race after a piddling amount of rain fell on the track.
WORD ELIMINATION:
1) b,c 2) a,b 3) d,e 4) c,e 5) a,c

1) *heated* (adjective)

Examples:
a)   The pair got into a heated debate over who was at fault for their accident.
b)   The jury witnessed the heated exchange between the prosecutor and the accused.
c)   Karen was heard yelling during a heated argument with her landlord.

Circle the correct meaning:

a) friendly   b) jovial   c) angry   d) brief   e) wordy

2) *peek* (noun)

Examples:
a)   She was caught taking a peek at her Christmas gifts before Christmas morning.
b)   The movie offered a rare peek into the lives of Tibetan Monks.
c)   "I just want to take a peek at the kids before we go," Mrs. Jones said to the babysitter.

Circle the correct meaning:

a) glance   b) shot   c) study   d) offer   e) discussion

3) *premature* (adjective)

Examples:
a)   Plans for a championship parade proved to be premature when the team lost its final game.
b)   The parents were unprepared for the premature arrival of their baby girl.
c)   The flights from Cuba arrived premature of their originally scheduled time of 2 pm.

Circle the correct meaning:

a) accurately   b) surprising   c) praise   d) early   e) together

4) *slim* (adjective)

Examples:
a)   Chances were slim that anyone survived the hotel fire.
b)   Hope for a turnaround in the economy was growing slim.
c)   Scientists reported a slim possibility a cure for the disease would be found.

Circle the correct meaning:

a) likely   b) doubtful   c) anticipated   d) certain   e) eager

5) *thud* (noun)

Examples:
a)   Witnesses report hearing a thud just before the train jumped the track.
b)   The boxer made a loud thud when he hit the mat.
c)   A broken piston caused the constant thud in the engine.

Circle the correct meaning:

a) speech   b) scream   c) hum   d) call   e) bang

FILL IN THE BLANKS:
Below are five sentences. Each contains a blank. Fill in the blank by using the appropriate word from this unit. Each word is used only once.

1) Predictions that interest rates would rise in 2002 proved to be ___________________.
2) The ___________________ on the roof was caused by a broken tree branch.
3) Larry took a ___________________ around the corner to see if Bill had arrived.
4) here was a ___________________ possibility the Buffalo Bills would make the playoffs.
5) After some ___________________ negotiations the two sides finally reached an agreement.

SYNONYM MATCHING:
On the left are words from this unit. Draw a line to the word on the right with the closest meaning.

1) heated   a) slight
2) peek   b) clunk
3) premature   c) intense
4) slim   d) too soon
5) thud   e) glimpse

SENTENCE BUILDING:
Assemble the scrambled clues below to form proper sentences.

1) between American/the site of/and British troops/Queenston was/a heated battle
2) Fans were hoping/of the movie/to get a/at the premier/peek at their/favorite stars
3) the entire/The premature/wheat crop/nearly destroyed/cold weather
4) getting rich from/was very slim/The chance of/the illegal scheme
5) The baby bird/trying to fly/made a/tiny thud/ground after/when it/hit the

WORD ELIMINATION:
Words from this unit are on the left. Five possible synonyms for each word are given below. Only three of the words are true synonyms. Circle the two words that do not belong.

1) heated	a) furious	b) composed	c) fierce	d) serene	e) irate
2) peek	a) examine	b) feel	c) look	d) gander	e) peer
3) premature	a) hasty	b) rash	c) early	d) unpaid	e) belated
4) slim	a) remote	b) improbable	c) confirmed	d) faint	e) expected
5) thud	a) silence	b) thump	c) bump	d) knock	e) quiet

ANSWER KEY:

CIRCLE THE CORRECT MEANING: 1) c 2) a 3) d 4) b 5) 3
FILL IN THE BLANKS: 1) premature 2) thud 3) pamper 4) slim 5) heated
SYNONYM MATCHING: 1) c 2) e 3) d 4) a 5) b
SENTENCE BUILDING:
1) Queenston was the site of a heated battle between American and British troops.
2) Fans were hoping to get a peek at their favorite stars at the premier of the movie.
3) The premature cold weather nearly destroyed the entire wheat crop.
4) The chance of getting rich from the illegal scheme was very slim.
5) The baby bird made a tiny thud when it hit the ground after trying to fly.
WORD ELIMINATION:
1) b,d 2) a,b 3) d,e 4) c,e 5) a,e

1) *aroma* (noun)

Examples:
a)   The air was thick with the aroma of freshly baked bread.
b)   The aroma of dad's famous beef stew made Tom hungry.
c)   The cheese had a mild aroma but a very strong taste.

Circle the correct meaning:

a) color   b) size   c) smell   d) thickness   e) texture

2) *cabal* (noun)

Examples:
a)   The cabal headed to the tournament included several members of the local boxing team.
b)   An obscure rule excluded women from being members of the secret cabal.
c)   The cabal was lead by a group of businessmen hoping to raise money for charity.

Circle the correct meaning:

a) group   b) vehicle   c) performance   d) parade   e) procession

3) *pesky* (adjective)

Examples:
a)   Opponents find Darcy Tucker a pesky hockey player to play against.
b)   A pesky swarm of grasshoppers was threatening to ruin the party.
c)   Adam could not get rid of his pesky cold.

Circle the correct meaning:

a) tiny   b) unfair   c) large   d) irritating   e) sudden

4) *rut* (noun)

Examples:
a)   Janice felt her life was in a rut and needed changing.
b)   Glenn and Laura agreed they had fallen into a rut when it came to meals.
c)   Opening your own business is one way to avoid the daily rut of going to work for someone else.

Circle the correct meaning:

a) spiral   b) dull routine   c) vacation   d) change   e) transformation

5) *spry* (adjective)

Examples:
a)   Mike was a spry old man who walked 5 miles every morning.
b)   Tessa had a spry imagination for a five-year-old child.
c)   The dog was remarkably spry for only having three legs.

Circle the correct meaning:

a) wobbly   b) smart   c) dark   d) empty   e) active

THE VOCABULARY DIET: UNIT 23

FILL IN THE BLANKS:
Below are five sentences. Each contains a blank. Fill in the blank by using the appropriate word from this unit. Each word is used only once.

1) The ___________________ dog next door continued to dig up Margaret's rose bushes.
2) The Middle Eastern ___________________ was lead by two oil barons.
3) Kelly looks much better since breaking out of her ___________________.
4) The ___________________ of apple strudel filtered out of the bakery window.
5) Marty was ___________________ on his feet when he hit the dance floor.

SYNONYM MATCHING:
On the left are words from this unit. Draw a line to the word on the right with the closest meaning.

1) aroma	a) scent
2) cabal	b) fixed way of life
3) pesky	c) agile
4) rut	d) infuriating
5) spry	e) faction

SENTENCE BUILDING:
Assemble the scrambled clues below to form proper sentences.

1) aroma that/of Italy/The soup/reminded her/had an
2) to join the/He decided not/cabal after/its mission/discovering the/goal of
3) They took/stains removed/the dress to/the pesky/the dry cleaners/to have
4) action films/making bad/the rut of/Movie studios/were in
5) looking for/the sales department/The company was/individuals to join/a few spry

WORD ELIMINATION:
Words from this unit are on the left. Five possible synonyms for each word are given below. Only three of the words are true synonyms. Circle the two words that do not belong.

1) aroma	a) design	b) odor	c) bouquet	d) volume	e) fragrance
2) cabal	a) gang	b) office	c) question	d) unit	e) coalition
3) pesky	a) annoying	b) aggravating	c) trying	d) quick	e) biting
4) rut	a) practice	b) smash	c) pattern	d) dirt	e) habit
5) spry	a) slow	b) energetic	c) lively	d) sluggish	e) agile

ANSWER KEY:
CIRCLE THE CORRECT MEANING: 1) c 2) a 3) d 4) b 5) e
FILL IN THE BLANKS: 1) pesky 2) cabal 3) rut 4) aroma 5) spry
SYNONYM MATCHING: 1) a 2) e 3) d 4) b 5) c
SENTENCE BUILDING:
1) The soup had an aroma that reminded her of Italy.
2) He decided not to join the cabal after discovering the goal of its mission.
3) They took the dress to the dry cleaners to have the pesky stains removed.
4) Movie studios were in the rut of making bad action films.
5) The company was looking for a few spry individuals to join the sales department.
WORD ELIMINATION:
1) a,d 2) b,c 3) d,e 4) b,d 5) a,d

1) *bulge* (noun)

Examples:
a)   The bulge in the tire made the bicycle unsafe for riding.
b)   The extra books in her backpack caused a large bulge.
c)   There was a huge bulge on the baby's forehead from banging his head into the door.

Circle the correct meaning:

a) hole   b) weight   c) addition   d) bump   e) obstacle

2) *campaign* (noun)

Examples:
a)   Steve was leading the campaign to have seatbelts installed on school buses.
b)   The candidates fought a bitter campaign for the vacant position in the mayor's office.
c)   The campaign against the developer ended with the sale of the property.

Circle the correct meaning:

a) fight   b) discussion   c) opposition   d) suggestion   e) meeting

3) *gloomy* (adjective)

Examples:
a)   The economic forecast for the new year was extremely gloomy.
b)   The drama was a gloomy piece about life on the farm.
c)   Brenda was feeling gloomy after the death of her beloved cat.

Circle the correct meaning:

a) special   b) intense   c) optimistic   d) depressed   e) available

4) *protocol* (noun)

Examples:
a)   It was standard protocol at the airport to check all suspicious packages.
b)   Military protocol called for all flags to be flown at half-mast.
c)   All students were required to attend the assembly as part of opening-day protocol.

Circle the correct meaning:

a) responsibility   b) procedure   c) example   d) suggestion   e) communication

5) *vendor* (noun)

Examples:
a)   Every vendor at the fruit market was required to pay a rental fee to the property owner.
b)   Kristen bought lunch from the hot-dog vendor.
c)   It was impossible to find a vendor still open on Christmas Day.

Circle the correct meaning:

a) person   b) spectator   c) viewer   d) purchase   e) merchant

THE VOCABULARY DIET: UNIT 24

FILL IN THE BLANKS:
Below are five sentences. Each contains a blank. Fill in the blank by using the appropriate word from this unit. Each word is used only once.

1) The _________________ to end smoking in restaurants put many people out of business.
2) The police officer was suspended for not following proper _________________.
3) The T-shirt _________________ outside the stadium was selling shirts for $10.00.
4) The _________________ in his jacket was an obvious indication he was hiding something.
5) Brian did not like classical music because he felt it was too _________________.

SYNONYM MATCHING:
On the left are words from this unit. Draw a line to the word on the right with the closest meaning.

1) bulge	a) seller
2) campaign	b) protuberance
3) gloomy	c) etiquette
4) protocol	d) crusade
5) vendor	e) dark

SENTENCE BUILDING:
Assemble the scrambled clues below to form proper sentences.

1) a long campaign/annual seal hunt/Greenpeace waged/to have the/banned forever
2) There was a/digest the rat/it tried to/huge bulge in/body as/the snake's
3) made it a/in the park/Severe cloud cover/very gloomy day
4) 911 in case/It was proper/protocol to dial/of an emergency
5) vendor because he/to sell goods/a proper license/Police arrested the/did not have

WORD ELIMINATION:
Words from this unit are on the left. Five possible synonyms for each word are given below. Only three of the words are true synonyms. Circle the two words that do not belong.

1) bulge	a) lump	b) prone	c) swell	d) flat	e) hump
2) campaign	a) surrender	b) movement	c) operation	d) struggle	e) ignore
3) gloomy	a) ominous	b) dismal	c) joyful	d) pleasing	e) miserable
4) protocol	a) confusion	b) custom	c) disorder	d) formality	e) courtesy
5) vendor	a) retailer	b) dealer	c) trader	d) package	e) commodity

ANSWER KEY:
CIRCLE THE CORRECT MEANING: 1) c 2) a 3) d 4) b 5) e
FILL IN THE BLANKS: 1) campaign 2) protocol 3) vendor 4) bulge 5) gloomy
SYNONYM MATCHING: 1) b 2) d 3) e 4) c 5) a
SENTENCE BUILDING:
1) Greenpeace waged a long campaign to have the annual seal hunt banned forever.
2) There was a huge bulge in the snake's body as it tried to digest the rat.
3) Severe cloud cover made it a very gloomy day in the park.
4) It was proper protocol to dial 911 in case of an emergency.
5) Police arrested the vendor because he did not have a proper license to sell goods.
WORD ELIMINATION:
1) b,d 2) a,e 3) c,d 4) a,c 5) d,e

1) *away* (adjective)

Examples:
a)   Mrs. Thompson noticed that Mark was away from his desk for over an hour.
b)   A cleaning company was hired to clean the house while the family was away.
c)   The robbery occurred while the security guard was away from her post.

Circle the correct meaning:

a) hiding   b) standing   c) sleeping   d) dining   e) gone

2) *blade* (noun)

Examples:
a)   A sharper blade was needed to cut through the leather strap.
b)   The lawnmower blade was dull and ineffective in the long grass.
c)   The blade of the razor was caked full of whiskers.

Circle the correct meaning:

a) cutting part   b) handle   c) body   d) front   e) design feature

3) *calm* (noun)

Examples:
a)   There was a sudden calm in the middle of the storm.
b)   The ceasefire brought a welcome calm to the streets of the war-torn city.
c)   The priest's presence brought calm to the grieving family.

Circle the correct meaning:

a) grief   b) conversation   c) peace   d) clamor   e) fury

4) *faithful* (adjective)

Examples:
a)   Mike received a gold watch for years of faithful service.
b)   He remained faithful to his vow of marriage until the day he died.
c)   David was a faithful follower of the Toronto Maple Leaf hockey team.

Circle the correct meaning:

a) doubtful   b) loyal   c) central   d) costly   e) dishonest

5) *horde* (noun)

Examples:
a)   The angry horde began to break windows and loot stores.
b)   The restaurant was unprepared for the horde of tourists that arrived on the bus.
c)   Sheila played host to a horde of children from her daughter's class.

Circle the correct meaning:

a) speaker   b) line   c) tangle   d) mob   e) number

FILL IN THE BLANKS:

Below are five sentences. Each contains a blank. Fill in the blank by using the appropriate word from this unit. Each word is used only once.

1) Police could not control the _________________ from climbing into the restricted area.
2) Martin Luther King brought _________________ to an era of enormous unrest.
3) Marsha was _________________ in Europe for the entire summer.
4) Horses have been _________________ servants to human beings for thousands of years.
5) The matador plunged his _________________ deep into the back of the charging bull.

SYNONYM MATCHING:

On the left are words from this unit. Draw a line to the word on the right with the closest meaning.

1) away   a) knife
2) blade   b) tranquility
3) calm   c) devoted
4) faithful   d) absent
5) horde   e) gang

SENTENCE BUILDING:

Assemble the scrambled clues below to form proper sentences.

1) piled up/porch while/on vacation/they were away/The mail/on the
2) The blade of/from solid gold/had been forged/the ancient sword
3) eerie calm in/the jungle while/There was an/the lions fed
4) It was/of finishing college/to her goal/to remain faithful/important to Diane
5) seats for the/attending the game/The stadium did/horde of fans/not have enough

WORD ELIMINATION:

Words from this unit are on the left. Five possible synonyms for each word are given below. Only three of the words are true synonyms. Circle the two words that do not belong.

1) away   a) near   b) missing   c) abroad   d) lacking   e) close
2) blade   a) dagger   b) machete   c) blunt   d) scalpel   e) branch
3) calm   a) riot   b) turmoil   c) quietness   d) stillness   e) serenity
4) faithful   a) trustworthy   b) crooked   c) fake   d) reliable   e) dependable
5) horde   a) crowd   b) group   c) lone   d) singular   e) multitude

---

ANSWER KEY:

CIRCLE THE CORRECT MEANING: 1) e 2) a 3) c 4) b 5) d
FILL IN THE BLANKS: 1) horde 2) calm 3) away 4) faithful 5) blade
SYNONYM MATCHING: 1) d 2) a 3) b 4) c 5) e
SENTENCE BUILDING:
1) The mail piled up on the porch while they were away on vacation.
2) The blade of the ancient sword had been forged from solid gold.
3) There was an eerie calm in the jungle while the lions fed.
4) It was important to Diane to remain faithful to her goal of finishing college.
5) The stadium did not have enough seats for the horde of fans attending the game.
WORD ELIMINATION:
1) a,e 2) c,e 3) a,b 4) b,c 5) c,d

1) *gutless* (adjective)

Examples:
a)   The engine on Bill's new car was too gutless to pull a trailer.
b)   Gutless people are not encouraged to enroll in the army.
c)   Manny was a gutless manager who could not make tough decisions.

Circle the correct meaning:

a) practical   b) worried   c) weak   d) abrupt   e) hollow

2) *hassle* (noun)

Examples:
a)   Earning a bigger salary is not always worth the hassle of having more responsibility at work.
b)   Clark encountered a hassle at the bank when he went in to cash his paycheck.
c)   It was a hassle having to drive the children to school each day.

Circle the correct meaning:

a) inconvenience   b) respect   c) surprise   d) duty   e) suggestion

3) *incline* (noun)

Examples:
a)   The marathon runners found it difficult to run up the incline.
b)   The car picked up speed as it rolled down the incline.
c)   The steep incline made it difficult to build a level foundation.

Circle the correct meaning:

a) horizon   b) staircase   c) countryside   d) slope   e) rollers

4) *snide* (adjective)

Examples:
a)   Ruth was upset by the snide remarks Debbie had made about her.
b)   The reporter printed some snide comments about Julia Robert's latest relationship.
c)   Martin had a snide look on his face as he approached the customer service desk.

Circle the correct meaning:

a) worried   b) nasty   c) caring   d) intimate   e) honest

5) *tolerable* (adjective)

Examples:
a)   The levels of dioxin in the water were considered tolerable for human consumption.
b)   The level of pain was tolerable enough for Greg to be able to continue playing.
c)   Sharon found her date's attitude to be barely tolerable.

Circle the correct meaning:

a) funny   b) concentrated   c) continuous   d) understandable   e) acceptable

FILL IN THE BLANKS:

Below are five sentences. Each contains a blank. Fill in the blank by using the appropriate word from this unit. Each word is used only once.

1) Justin warned his daughter not to make any _________________ comments about his date.
2) The Internet allows you to buy things without the _________________ of leaving home.
3) Braden was too _________________ to tell Dani the truth about his feelings for Dakota.
4) Bernie could not maneuver his wheelchair up the steep _________________.
5) Driving while under the influence of alcohol is not considered _________________ behavior.

SYNONYM MATCHING:

On the left are words from this unit. Draw a line to the word on the right with the closest meaning.

1) gutless	a) cowardly
2) hassle	b) bother
3) incline	c) slant
4) snide	d) mean
5) tolerable	e) allowable

SENTENCE BUILDING:

Assemble the scrambled clues below to form proper sentences.

1) The snow blower/the heavy snow/from the sidewalk/was too gutless/to remove
2) a new/Shopping for/becoming a/car was/major hassle
3) made about Bert/There was no/Oscar had/truth to the/snide remarks
4) built to transport/of the incline/the top/The elevator was/passengers to
5) found the scent/She did not/of cigars tolerable/smoke although she

WORD ELIMINATION:

Words from this unit are on the left. Five possible synonyms for each word are given below. Only three of the words are true synonyms. Circle the two words that do not belong.

1) gutless	a) afraid	b) brave	c) alert	d) fearful	e) timid
2) hassle	a) dispute	b) problem	c) struggle	d) solution	e) result
3) incline	a) field	b) hill	c) rise	d) grade	e) plain
4) snide	a) unpleasant	b) amusing	c) unkind	d) lovely	e) hurtful
5) tolerable	a) bearable	b) endurable	c) envious	d) reasonable	e) superior

---

ANSWER KEY:

CIRCLE THE CORRECT MEANING: 1) c 2) a 3) d 4) b 5) e
FILL IN THE BLANKS: 1) snide 2) hassle 3) gutless 4) incline 5) tolerable
SYNONYM MATCHING: 1) a 2) b 3) c 4) d 5) e
SENTENCE BUILDING:
1) The snow blower was too gutless to remove the heavy snow from the sidewalk.
2) Shopping for a new car was becoming a major hassle.
3) There was no truth to the snide remarks Oscar had made about Bert.
4) The elevator was built to transport passengers to the top of the incline.
5) She did not smoke although she found the scent of cigars tolerable.
WORD ELIMINATION:
1) b,c 2) d,e 3) a,e 4) b,d 5) c,e

1) *blunder* (noun)

Examples:
a)   The blunder in accounting cost the company over one million dollars.
b)   The quarterback made a major blunder that cost the team the victory.
c)   Paul corrected his blunder before anyone noticed.

Circle the correct meaning:

a) calculation   b) decision   c) choice   d) mistake   e) variety

2) *demise* (noun)

Examples:
a)   The demise of the company was the result of bad management.
b)   The eventual demise of the show was scheduled for December.
c)   The dog met an untimely demise after running in front of the car.

Circle the correct meaning:

a) end   b) success   c) schedule   d) turmoil   e) chaos

3) *hydro* (noun)

Examples:
a)   The electrician was needed to hook up the hydro for the sound system.
b)   It is important to shut off the hydro before working on the fuse box.
c)   There was not enough hydro to run operate the appliances.

Circle the correct meaning:

a) extension   b) power   c) ladder   d) television   e) circuit

4) *infant* (noun)

Examples:
a)   The clothes were so small only an infant could wear them.
b)   A special seat is required to transport an infant in a car.
c)   She cradled the tiny infant in her arms.

Circle the correct meaning:

a) animal   b) object   c) baby   d) teenager   e) student

5) *putrid* (adjective)

Examples:
a)   There was a putrid smell coming from the canning-factory smokestack.
b)   The shoreline was covered in the putrid flesh of dead fish.
c)   The toxic chemical container was overflowing with putrid waste.

Circle the correct meaning:

a) oily   b) thick   c) liquid   d) colorful   e) rotten

FILL IN THE BLANKS:
Below are five sentences. Each contains a blank. Fill in the blank by using the appropriate word from this unit. Each word is used only once.

1) The roller coaster operator told Mitch he could not take an _________________ on the ride.
2) A garbage truck overturned and spilled _________________ waste onto the highway.
3) Matt double-checked all the figures to avoid a mathematical _________________.
4) Many were saddened by the sudden _________________ of hamburger mogul Dave Thomas.
5) Duane's _________________ was cut off because he did not pay his utility bill.

SYNONYM MATCHING:
On the left are words from this unit. Draw a line to the word on the right with the closest meaning.

1)	blunder	a) end
2)	demise	b) newborn
3)	hydro	c) rancid
4)	infant	d) gaffe
5)	putrid	e) electricity

SENTENCE BUILDING:
Assemble the scrambled clues below to form proper sentences.

1) The substitute teacher's/in geography/a higher mark/blunder cost William
2) demise of dinosaurs/There are many/caused the final/theories on what
3) for children to/where hydro runs/It is dangerous/through overhead wires/play in areas
4) Dr. Ballyk told/their tiny infant/perfect health/was in/the young parents
5) putrid smell/Health authorities/could not determine/the origin/of the

WORD ELIMINATION:
Words from this unit are on the left. Five possible synonyms for each word are given below. Only three of the words are true synonyms. Circle the two words that do not belong.

1)	blunder	a) fix	b) repair	c) error	d) oversight	e) faux pas
2)	demise	a) passing	b) termination	c) birth	d) departure	e) beginning
3)	hydro	a) voltage	b) air	c) current	d) bulb	e) energy
4)	infant	a) father	b) sibling	c) child	d) toddler	e) tot
5)	putrid	a) fresh	b) decomposed	c) rank	d) decayed	e) fragrant

---

ANSWER KEY:

CIRCLE THE CORRECT MEANING: 1) d 2) a 3) b 4) c 5) e
FILL IN THE BLANKS: 1) infant 2) putrid 3) blunder 4) demise 5) hydro
SYNONYM MATCHING: 1) d 2) a 3) e 4) b 5) c
SENTENCE BUILDING:
1) The substitute teacher's blunder cost William a higher mark in geography.
2) There are many theories on what caused the final demise of dinosaurs.
3) It is dangerous for children to play in areas where hydro runs through overhead wires.
4) Dr. Ballyk told the young parents their tiny infant was in perfect health.
5) Health authorities could not determine the origin of the putrid smell.
WORD ELIMINATION:
1) a,b 2) c,e 3) b,d 4) a,b 5) a,e

1) *accidental* (adjective)

Examples:
a)   The accidental discovery of the missing gene made the scientists famous.
b)   If not for their accidental meeting in France the couple would never have married.
c)   Any resemblance to current members of parliament is purely accidental.

Circle the correct meaning:

a) coincidental   b) planned   c) scheduled   d) expected   e) required

2) *chat* (noun)

Examples:
a)   Mr. Taylor sat his children down for a long chat about their grandmother.
b)   The phone chat with Reggie lasted over two hours.
c)   The two counselors had a casual chat in the school staff room.

Circle the correct meaning:

a) meal   b) conversation   c) argument   d) fight   e) description

3) *disarming* (adjective)

Examples:
a)   Robert F. Kennedy Jr. has the same disarming personality that made his father popular.
b)   Cameron's disarming good looks made him popular with the ladies at the tennis club.
c)   It was a disarming love story about two high-school sweethearts.

Circle the correct meaning:

a) disturbing   b) foreign   c) charming   d) shocking   e) troubling

4) *gap* (noun)

Examples:
a)   There was a lengthy gap between marching bands in the annual parade.
b)   The President waved to the crowd during a gap in the action at the football game.
c)   A satellite malfunction caused a two-hour gap in televised programming.

Circle the correct meaning:

a) crowd   b) procession   c) continuation   d) interruption   e) extension

5) *slight* (adjective)

Examples:
a)   The painters spilled a slight bit of paint on the carpet.
b)   The difference in the paintings was so slight it was hard to tell one was a forgery.
c)   A slight trace of frozen water was discovered on the distant planet.

Circle the correct meaning:

a) considerable   b) many   c) visible   d) generous   e) small

FILL IN THE BLANKS:

Below are five sentences. Each contains a blank. Fill in the blank by using the appropriate word from this unit. Each word is used only once.

1) The tired jury members appreciated the _________________ in courtroom proceedings.
2) The fact that Cheryl's cooking was so good was considered purely _________________.
3) The officer was so _________________ that Sharon confessed to the crime immediately.
4) The promotions directors invited Mike into his office for a brief _________________.
5) Eric Lindros suffered a _________________ concussion during the hockey game.

SYNONYM MATCHING:

On the left are words from this unit. Draw a line to the word on the right with the closest meaning.

1) accidental   a) appealing
2) chat   b) little
3) disarming   c) chance
4) gap   d) pause
5) slight   e) talk

SENTENCE BUILDING:

Assemble the scrambled clues below to form proper sentences.

1) game winning goal/an accidental tip/Mark admitted his/was scored with/of the puck
2) discuss the matter/his lawyer to/brief chat with/Theo scheduled a
3) around children/She was always/disarming manner/Stanley had/impressed with the
4) six meters/There was a/fence of approximately/gap in the
5) There was a/beef stew/slight taste/in the/of basil

WORD ELIMINATION:

Words from this unit are on the left. Five possible synonyms for each word are given below. Only three of the words are true synonyms. Circle the two words that do not belong.

1) accidental	a) fluky	b) unintentional	c) designed	d) unforeseen	e) intended
2) chat	a) silence	b) listen	c) dialogue	d) discussion	e) exchange
3) disarming	a) magnetic	b) irresistible	c) appealing	d) annoying	e) trying
4) gap	a) complete	b) space	c) lull	d) break	e) entire
5) slight	a) unimportant	b) chief	c) tiny	d) major	e) slim

ANSWER KEY:

CIRCLE THE CORRECT MEANING: 1) a 2) b 3) c 4) d 5) e
FILL IN THE BLANKS: 1) gap 2) accidental 3) disarming 4) chat 5) slight
SYNONYM MATCHING: 1) c 2) e 3) a 4) d 5) b
SENTENCE BUILDING:
1) Mark admitted his game winning goal was scored with an accidental tip of the puck.
2) Theo scheduled a brief chat with his lawyer to discuss the matter.
3) She was always impressed with the disarming manner Stanley had with children.
4) There was a gap in the fence of approximately six meters.
5) There was a slight taste of basil in the beef stew.
WORD ELIMINATION:
1) c,e 2) a,b 3) d,e 4) a,e 5) b,d

1) *art* (noun)

Examples:
a)   Chef Robert's great art is making delicate pastry.
b)   She worked as a photographer but her real art was graphic design.
c)   Timothy's art was glass blowing.

Circle the correct meaning:

a) talent   b) choice   c) job   d) career   e) business

2) *caution* (noun)

Examples:
a)   They approached the subject of his divorce with extreme caution.
b)   The caution she took when changing the baby revealed her loving nature.
c)   Negotiations were entered with caution because of recent tensions between the two countries.

Circle the correct meaning:

a) force   b) vigor   c) prudence   d) brutality   e) energy

3) *district* (noun)

Examples:
a)   Senator Williamson spent the weekend campaigning in the district closest to his house.
b)   There were too many traffic accidents happening in the district near the school.
c)   The district was bounded in the north by the highway.

Circle the correct meaning:

a) field   b) avenue   c) lot   d) region   e) building

4) *episode* (noun)

Examples:
a)   The entire episode at the bank lasted for three hours.
b)   The episode at the restaurant was a complete embarrassment for Michael.
c)   It was an episode from her past she was trying to forget.

Circle the correct meaning:

a) lodging   b) reservation   c) reminder   d) hassle   e) incident

5) *quarrel* (noun)

Examples:
a)   The family had endured a lifelong quarrel with the neighbor.
b)   They both realized the quarrel was starting to affect their relationship.
c)   Greg was willing to take up the quarrel with the city over zoning bylaws.

Circle the correct meaning:

a) delivery   b) dispute   c) friendship   d) alliance   e) partnership

FILL IN THE BLANKS:

Below are five sentences. Each contains a blank. Fill in the blank by using the appropriate word from this unit. Each word is used only once.

1) Their _________________ was with the car dealer who sold them the faulty vehicle.
2) Experts blamed the entire _________________ on unruly protestors.
3) Drew had a real _________________ for negotiating contracts.
4) The nurse administered the needle with _________________ so the child would not cry.
5) The house was located in a rundown _________________ of the city.

SYNONYM MATCHING:

On the left are words from this unit. Draw a line to the word on the right with the closest meaning.

1) art		a) squabble
2) caution		b) affair
3) district		c) neighborhood
4) episode		d) carefulness
5) quarrel		e) skill

SENTENCE BUILDING:

Assemble the scrambled clues below to form proper sentences.

1) in need/His art was/help those/bringing people/together to
2) moving ahead/the proper treatment/ensure she received/Doctors were/with caution to
3) was destroyed by/An entire district/the unexpected tornado/of the state
4) video cameras/The entire/close-circuit/episode was/captured by
5) They patched up/an apology and/their quarrel with/a hand shake

WORD ELIMINATION:

Words from this unit are on the left. Five possible synonyms for each word are given below. Only three of the words are true synonyms. Circle the two words that do not belong.

1) art	a) knack	b) clumsy	c) flair	d) inept	e) expertise
2) caution	a) regard	b) concern	c) thought	d) casual	e) forgetful
3) district	a) home	b) dwelling	c) area	d) borough	e) ward
4) episode	a) volume	b) event	c) occurrence	d) occasion	e) entire
5) quarrel	a) argument	b) union	c) harmony	d) tiff	e) clash

ANSWER KEY:

CIRCLE THE CORRECT MEANING: 1) a 2) c 3) d 4) e 5) b
FILL IN THE BLANKS: 1) quarrel 2) episode 3) art 4) caution 5) district
SYNONYM MATCHING: 1) e 2) d 3) c 4) b 5) a
SENTENCE BUILDING:
1) His art was bringing people together to help those in need.
2) Doctors were moving ahead with caution to ensure she received the proper treatment.
3) An entire district of the state was destroyed by the unexpected tornado.
4) The entire episode was captured by close-circuit video cameras.
5) They patched up their quarrel with an apology and a hand shake.
WORD ELIMINATION:
1) b,d 2) d,e 3) a,b 4) a,e 5) b,c

1) *danger* (noun)

Examples:
a)   There is a danger the dam might collapse if the water level continues to rise.
b)   Falling from the high wire is always a danger for circus tightrope walkers.
c)   When investing in the stock market there is always the danger the stocks could lose money.

Circle the correct meaning:

a) belief   b) risk   c) idea   d) principal   e) injury

2) *division* (noun)

Examples:
a)   He worked in the sporting goods division of the local hardware store.
b)   Kelly got transferred to the manufacturing division at the company.
c)   Melissa had to send money to the license division of the ministry of transportation.

Circle the correct meaning:

a) floor   b) management   c) department   d) file   e) category

3) *frequently* (adjective)

Examples:
a)   They visited the cemetery frequently to lay flowers next to Barbara's grave.
b)   The roof was leaking more frequently now that the spring rains had started.
c)   The movie theatre frequently gave its patrons free popcorn during their movie screenings.

Circle the correct meaning:

a) never   b) rarely   c) uncommonly   d) unlikely   e) often

4) *jagged* (adjective)

Examples:
a)   She ripped her nylons after catching them on a jagged piece of plastic.
b)   The saw had a jagged edge that ripped through the wood.
c)   Keenan was nervous about skiing down the jagged slope.

Circle the correct meaning:

a) uneven   b) smooth   c) shiny   d) blunt   e) metal

5) *quiz* (noun)

Examples:
a)   The teacher announced the class would receive a surprise quiz.
b)   On his last quiz Justin answered every question correctly.
c)   The students had to receive a mark of at least 60% on the quiz in order to pass the course.

Circle the correct meaning:

a) buzz   b) speaker   c) assignment   d) test   e) subject

FILL IN THE BLANKS:

Below are five sentences. Each contains a blank. Fill in the blank by using the appropriate word from this unit. Each word is used only once.

1) Melissa stayed up all night studying for her geography ___________________.
2) The floor of the cave was covered in long ___________________ rocks.
3) There is always a ___________________ of falling off when learning to ride a bicycle.
4) The family ___________________ liked to dine out together at the local restaurant.
5) Ford Motor Company announced layoffs in the truck manufacturing ___________________.

SYNONYM MATCHING:

On the left are words from this unit. Draw a line to the word on the right with the closest meaning.

1) danger   a) rigid
2) division   b) section
3) frequently   c) exam
4) jagged   d) possibility
5) quiz   e) many times

SENTENCE BUILDING:

Assemble the scrambled clues below to form proper sentences.

1) think of the/danger they might/Fighter pilots rarely/be shot down
2) division at Microsoft/new computer programming/Mike was hired/to manage the
3) seizures happened/cold weather/The dog's/more frequently/during the
4) hand on the/the broken glass/He cut his/jagged edge of
5) One of the/difficult math problem/quiz included a/questions on the

WORD ELIMINATION:

Words from this unit are on the left. Five possible synonyms for each word are given below. Only three of the words are true synonyms. Circle the two words that do not belong.

1) danger   a) luck   b) fate   c) likelihood   d) chance   e) probability
2) division   a) group   b) branch   c) consumer   d) employee   e) sector
3) frequently   a) habitually   b) seldom   c) constantly   d) rarely   e) repeatedly
4) jagged   a) flat   b) rough   c) pointy   d) sharp   e) glossy
5) quiz   a) inquiry   b) questioning   c) knowledge   d) assessment   e) learn

---

ANSWER KEY:

CIRCLE THE CORRECT MEANING: 1) b 2) c 3) e 4) a 5) d
FILL IN THE BLANKS: 1) quiz 2) jagged 3) danger 4) frequently 5) division
SYNONYM MATCHING: 1) d 2) b 3) e 4) a 5) c
SENTENCE BUILDING:
1) Fighter pilots rarely think of the danger they might be shot down.
2) Mike was hired to manage the new computer programming division at Microsoft.
3) The dog's seizures happened more frequently during the cold weather.
4) He cut his hand on the jagged edge of the broken glass.
5) One of the questions on the quiz included a difficult math problem.
WORD ELIMINATION:
1) a,b 2) c,d 3) b,d 4) a,e 5) c,e

Made in the USA
Monee, IL
07 July 2026